Wind and Tide

Wind and Tide

✵

An Introduction to Cruising in Pure Sailing Craft

Jerome FitzGerald

Writers Club Press
San Jose New York Lincoln Shanghai

Wind and Tide
An Introduction to Cruising in Pure Sailing Craft

Writers Club Press
an imprint of iUniverse, Inc.

For information address:
iUniverse, Inc.
5220 S. 16th St., Suite 200
Lincoln, NE 68512
www.iuniverse.com

ISBN: 0-595-21733-8

Printed in the United States of America

This is an Oar Club book:

This book is dedicated to those who sail and appreciate the beauty inherent in sailing. This book is dedicated as well to promoting the skill, character, and seamanship displayed by those who sail in its traditional fashion—without the aid of engines. This book affirms the rigors of true sailing—the attentiveness they demand and the strength they contest—as rewards: This is what makes the experience meaningful. We cannot imagine demeaning our experience by making it trivial or common. That does not mean that we demand that we cross oceans (though some do) or rashly brave storms (though some have) but rather that we do what we do, in a manner real and meaningful, and eschew that which is not. Perhaps fifty percent of seamanship occurs within fifty feet of a dock…

Contents

Introduction

The need to write this book was created by trying to teach a class on "sailing" and the search for a text to use . .

There are a lot of books on the shelves that have something to do with sailing—but the "sailing" we're going to be talking about in this book seems to have become a bit of a lost art. The "sailing" world has been well marketed and merchandised—boats are bought off the line just like the new model of cars—boats are designed to be as accessible and turn–key as possible. Sailing has become more accessibly casual. This has created a new kind of yachtsman—one who has by and large forgotten many of the skills and lessons that a yachtsman of fifty years ago might have had. Fifty years ago it took more ability and commitment to sail than it does today. The yachtsman of fifty years ago learned from this commitment—whether he wanted to or not. Today this is no longer the case. The yachtsman of today has not felt the need to learn the skills of the past—*he hasn't had the need.* The influence of the "work boat" world of sailing—that might have served as an example to the yachtsman of years past—with all its practicality, functionality, and knowledge has all but disappeared. We have those, in places, which try to keep these nautical arts alive in one forum or another—but more often than not the efforts take the form of exhibition rather than demonstrations of viability.

This is not to be a book of academic interest. This is to be a very practical text with the intent of introducing the reader to the practical skills of handling a sailboat. A sailboat, as defined in this text, is a boat powered by sail. It is not a powerboat. It is not a power–assisted sail craft. It is powered by sail, and controlled by the human beings that ride upon it—not synthetic electromechanical crew. Some would say that this "sailing purism" is at best an esoteric exercise—exhibition

1

again—but we say it is not. There are _very practical reasons_ why one might—upon choosing a sailboat with which to see the far places of the world—decide to choose a pure sailing craft. There might be more reason for it all the time...

This book is written for one who has learned some about sailing, has done some sailing, and is perhaps considering taking up cruising or perhaps purchasing a boat. It is not a primer—it assumes the reader has some knowledge of the basics of sail. This book will likely be of great use to this individual. This book is also written from the perspective of the coastal or inland sailor—as it presents the most complicated tactical problems that a sailor faces—and teaches the most pertinent points.

So while not a "primer"—for many this book will be an introduction. It is an introduction to sailing in its true form, and the attitude sailing requires. Sailing is not learned by power–assisted voyaging, nor is it learned by maneuvering around a few yellow buoys in a bay. These teach something, of course, but what these activities teach are certainly not a complete representation of the activity we call "sailing." This book is has no pretense to be complete either. Not intended to be comprehensive, it is intended to be facilitating. If we raise issues that are often ignored—and to point the way to discovering the solutions to these issues, by oneself and one's experience—one may, through time, be on one's way to learn what sailing is all about. That is the goal of this book. There is no way to learn to sail but by doing it...

Why Choose to Cruise in an Engineless Sailboat?

Let's get right to it: Why would anyone want to "cruise" without an engine? Perhaps what we should ask first is why people would want to "cruise" at all. What is the activity of cruising anyway?

Commonly, I suppose, "cruising" means traveling in a semi–exploratory fashion in boats. It is a different activity than simply traveling—the term does specifically specify the involvement of water travel. Historically, this has also suggested sailboats rather than power—although this has certainly changed in recent years. Why the water travel? Perhaps the symbolism is the key. Perhaps one could suggest that water travel necessitates a higher level of participation with one's environment than many other forms of travel might—like riding in an airplane or on a bus, or careening down the freeway in a motor-home. There is an implicit value in this; to say that while one *could* go to island X, for example, by taking a flight, the "cruiser" who travels by means of sail wants to go there in a matter that *teaches, tests, and proves something*. This also suggests that that if one really wants to experience something, then one must have a bit of an investment in it. One might even go so far to say that the quality of the experience is relative and *dependant* on the amount of effort involved. An experience may be had in a manner so much more meaningful than another—that it might casually resemble—that it may *no longer even be the same <u>type</u> of experience*. If one walks over a mountain rather than drives around it, one sees indeed a <u>*different*</u> mountain. Most of us would suggest a greater mountain at that.

We can reasonably suggest that "sailing" is, in many ways, and perhaps even fundamentally, an "aesthetic" activity at its core. For "cruising under sail" to be meaningful—more than a mere lark or some lackadaisical diversion for unimaginative folks with too much time and money on their hands—it must fit within a certain symbolic framework. One is drawn to the activity because one finds it appealing—this suggests a lack somewhere that wants to be filled. If one ignores this symbolic framework—if one ignores the stimulus that gave rise to the effort—the resultant experience will certainly be less than satisfying.

I do not think that anyone with sense can say that there is much aesthetically pleasing or symbolically constructive about the sort of people that blast around in huge motor yachts. While this activity obviously appeals to a certain tasteless segment of the population—its popularity is no testament to the quality of the experience. Experience requires sensitivity: Power–boating demands one shut one's senses off. It is necessary within the experience to ignore the noise, the vibration, the ride of the boat. It is necessary too to ignore the smoke, the oil slick, and the beach erosion that one's passage causes. It is necessary too to ignore the statement of such a passage: belittlement of the local peoples homes and environment as secondary to one's own jollies, and to frankly discard any care about meaningful interaction with these people. Power–boating demands, then, that one be a sort of person with poor awareness. It demands of its adherents little, except that they be some sort of semi–functional deaf–mute idiot...a demand met and all too often evinced by their level of boat–handling skill and shore side behavior.

Some people with more taste claim to still cruise what passes for "sailboats," although this number is dwindling in comparison to their noisy bastard cousins. "Sailing," I will insist, however, has become an activity seldom practiced. Many "cruisers" who claim to "sail" today gloat with pride if their passages make the fifty percent mark in terms of their ratio of sail miles covered to power. This has become reasonable. Not only this, it has also become reasonable to expect to only sail when it is convenient, and the wind and weather are within a very narrow range of conditions. When seamanship is called for, or when speed drops below an arbitrary number—indeed when most perform the very act of setting sail—the engine comes on. These boats are designed, crewed and "cruised" in a manner that makes "sailing" impossible, thus they demand auxiliary power. People say it is only reasonable to have an engine on board a "sailboat." Reasonable? This engine removes the greater need for seamanship, for knowledge, even for *personal invest-ment;* thus the resultant experience is fundamentally changed. Is it reasonable to ignore the fundamental reason why one might want to sail at all?

Most people one meets are avid "motor–sailors." Most people have "motor–sailor" craft where the auxiliary engine is *critical* to the function of the vessel. It is necessary for propulsion, as well as for the power to drive convenience systems. It is the artificial crew that allows sail changes to be made. It is the hands that set and haul the anchor. It is the eyes that keep watch. This is obviously the case. This is indeed typical and expected.

Yet if you were to call one of these "sailors" a "motor–sailor" or refer to the boat as a "motor–sailer," as it *obviously is*—by every potential definition—most of these "motor–sailors" would bristle. They would take this as an insult.

Why should this be troublesome? Either one "sails" a "sailboat" or one does not. This is pretty simple concept. If one "cruises" under sail—then one is a cruising "sailor." Again, not a difficult concept. Why then do not most people freely admit they are "motorsailors" and not "sailors?" Why do people get hot under the collar when called a "motorsailor?" Why should this be construed as an insult? *Because we all recognize that it takes more skill and ability to handle a sailboat under sail than it does to handle a motorsailor, and we respect that.* We recognize that it takes more investment to make passages under sail than it does under power–assisted sail. We recognize that a person who has the will, ability, skill, and stamina to do so has more will, ability, skill, and stamina than one that does not. We understand that a "sailor'" is in many ways a more skilled human being than is a "motorsailor." Understanding this, many people *do desire* to be sailors and to sail. Unfortunately, however, many of these same people do not care to make the investment necessary, nor they do not have an interest in the amount of sweat and effort involved. Still, they desire the status of skill and so have learned to merely *presume* to be "sailors." They pretend. Thus the insult of inherent in the term "motorsailor." It calls a spade a spade.

This is fraud. We all know this. We, once again, are drawn to this activity for a reason: a lack. If we do not fulfill this lack—our activity is a failure. Among those that fail—it is common to preach the method of failure for it masks one's own. To preach failure is dangerous. Yet this is what drives the boating world…We know all too often the silliness of our activity—hence the vast array of "boat things" that we purchase and bolt to our boats in an endeavor to make them appear more "serious" or more "seaworthy"—as if a "motor–sailer" needed more gear to become more a "sailboat."

"Cruising under sail" is an aesthetic activity which ends can only be met by aesthetic means. Sailboats—straight sailers now—are aesthetic to their essence. They are motive shapes—a complex collection of curves that creates motion out of force by sheer being—it is difficult indeed to find a creation of the hand of man that is as exquisite an example of form following function following the forces of nature that equals the sailboat. We sense this—it is an appropriate vehicle for an aesthetic task. Our senses need not rebel at its proximity. It is an appropriate ally in our endeavor.

It would be difficult to argue that activities that challenge our skills and encourage development of strength and character are *not* good for us. In "cruising" again, we agree it is fair to say that the "challenge" of the activity is an inherent part of the quality of the experience. I must point out, however, "challenge" is a relative concept, and what might be routine for one might be high adventure for others. We see that in the adventures many have simply getting on and off the dock. Yet there is no inherent virtue in incompetence—even though I admit incompetence might often make things more exciting. Neither is there inherent virtue in not evincing any progression in one's abilities—for one who has spent a few years on the water, passage–making in a powered craft must be nothing if not simply boring and unrewarding. We do not feel a sense of pride (I hope) in successfully driving our cars fifty miles without mishap—although once in our lives, years ago, driving was high adventure.

Sailing is not like that at all. Each passage is a new experience. The number of variables one must take into consideration in making a successful passage under sail—variables the presence of the engine makes insignificant—makes every passage a challenge. While after time an acquisition of local knowledge may diminish the level of adventure in one's native grounds—there is always the next fifty miles of water to explore and its particular characteristics. It is simply much more difficult to make good passages under sail. It is mentally tougher and physically tougher. Those who eschew the engine certainly will become mentally stronger and physically tougher as a result.

The purest and most rewarding form of travel must be walking. This is difficult to do on the water. For those of us drawn to sea, sailing is the next purest thing. Some of us need desperately to escape the triviality of daily life. Engines make trivial.

The degree to which engines make power–assisted sailing trivial is disguised. Sailing, in good conditions, takes nearly no ability at all. One can log off a thousand miles under the keel with hardly touching a sheet. One could be asleep, or dead even, and the boat would have continued along its way. While this sort of sailing is pleasant, it is certainly not challenging, nor does it teach or demand much of the sailor aboard. No, sailing, and "seamanship" does not so much involve the thousand mile passage in ideal conditions, although it is involved in producing it—"seamanship" involves much more that hundred feet of contrary current off the point that one cannot make way against. It involves getting under sail in good manner and entering a harbor with proficiency after a passage. People like to think of themselves as a 80%

sailor, and a 20% motor–sailor—although such a ratio is dangerously close to a "yachtsman's gale." They like to think in terms of hours underway, or miles underway, for this ratio. This disguises or belittles the fact—that without the engine, had they encountered that hundred feet of the contrary current and not been able to deal with it—even after a thousand miles, they still would have *failed* to make port. Properly, then, their ratio should be expressed as 100% power–assisted sail, as they would have been helpless without the engine. It is important to note that in any activity that is judged by its completion, a 1% failure means a 100% failure…Let us be 100% sailors…

Moving on to other issues, let me start by saying that not many things make me cringe as much as seeing a "think green" sticker on the back of a car. It would be funny as a joke—appalling in reality. I cannot understand the mentality of those who would deliberately seek out pristine places in the quest of good experience and defile these places with their presence. Make no mistake about it—diesel engines are terrible polluters. Many people don't care. My only assumption about this is that those that don't suffer from the damage that they cause must be significantly insensitive—I'm not sure what these insensitive people are accomplishing on the water other than damage. If one is insensitive to the damage, they must also be insensitive to the experience. Are they having a good time? In a trivial way?

As I see it, and as I think reasonable, thinking people do—ecological and environmental issues are secondary issues rather than primary ones. This is to say that we see an ecologically beneficial lifestyle as a fundamental aspect of "right living." For any healthy human being, "Right Living" is the first task—environmentalism follows. We might even feel this is seldom the case in what we see; seldom the case in the shill cries we hear for "save the 'X'". As the careful and reasoned mind sees it—our ecological responsibility is not nearly as simple as many would have us believe. The claim that we often hear—that the "environment" is being "destroyed"—this is an intellectually indefensible claim. It is a spiritual/religious claim that begs a lot of questions—and like all spiritual/religious claims—its presumptuous presuppositions breed much contention. The environment is indeed <u>not</u> being destroyed, but it <u>is</u> unquestionably being *altered,* and altered in a manner that is quite likely to be damaging to many species—including humans. From a holistic sense, however, for life itself—most of which is comprised in the form of some worm or bug—very little of note is likely to occur.

But for myself, since I don't flourish under high levels of ultra–violet radiation, nor does my system effectively metabolize PCB's—I think I am in for a world of hurt. I am indeed disturbed by the environmental trends I see. So then, disaffirming the spiritual/religious arguments towards conservation, I will affirm some highly personal and selfish ones. Every organism that lives has an understandable desire not to see its home, habit, health or life destroyed, no matter whether it is cognitive of the fact or not. Also, no matter whether cognitive of the fact or not, every species clambers after the propagation, survival, and elevation of itself. This is inherent in life, and necessary to its existence. To say that life seeks itself is a tautology: would life possibly seek death?

Everything that lives, as well, creates a bit of corruption and stink around it as it moves through life. This is another inescapable fact of existence. Nothing runs at 100% efficiency. Entropy is a fundamental reality of the universe. The issue is not IF we corrupt our home but whether we do so in such a way that corrupts us with it as well. There is a danger to that end contained in life. Large numbers of species—yeast, carp, and humans all come to mind—show a tendency to run unrestrained, to eat themselves to death and die in their own excrement. I'd like to think that humans are more farsighted than yeast. Time will tell.

Stating that scale of consumption is the key issue—everything that lives is entitled to a little bit—we have an enormous problem on our hands. This problem is that the world is a zero sum game. With a finite amount of space and resources—as population increases, all get poorer. This is inescapable. When one member of the species gathers a disproportionate amount of wealth and resources, the others suffer for it. This too is inescapable. Although the richness and abundance of the past obscured and took the edge off of this reality—richness and abundance is no longer the case. It is time to admit that the acquisition of disproportionate wealth is **violence**, indistinguishable from any other sort of violence in the harm it causes. Indeed we judge violence <u>by</u> the amount of harm it causes. It would be difficult to find a greater source of woe than that caused by our rampant materialism…

We have a very entrenched, erroneous, and self–indulgent view towards wealth in our culture. We'd like to believe that the acquisition of wealth is somehow related to natural selection—that the financially successful are entitled by nature to consume—that somehow a "survival of the fittest" model applies and justifies materialism and consumption. This is, upon critique, obviously false. The wealthy are NOT our fittest. They are indeed the most feeble, least fit representatives of our species, requiring the highest amount of material maintenance and producing the least with it. They are the most fragile as well, most likely to fail if their support is withdrawn. They are dependent, in fact, on the strength of the truly productive masses; without them they would have nothing. There is little, if nothing, admirable about the affluent; even if we admire their means we are more often awestruck by how little is accomplished with it.

If not "survival of the fittest", then what? A sickly destructive parasitism? It is hard for me to describe my feeling—the terms thief, cannibal, vampire come to mind—but I might even find some virtue in these. What then? The self–destructively violent? Is there anything wrong, even, with violence? I'm not sure I can argue that either. What I CAN offer with integrity is this: I affirm life. I observe that there are actions and attitudes—lifestyles as well—which contribute to and promote life and those that do not, both *personally* and *globally*. There may even be violence that promotes life and strengthens the species—as I said, I won't argue against that possibility. What I cannot even imagine as defensible, however, or attractive in any way, is a promotion of the unhealthy, unviable, unattractive, and few—at the expense of the many—and I mean many in an interspecieal sense.

If one is to affirm life (and the only alternative I see is to jump off a bridge) one must affirm the welfare of the species as a whole and that within the system that supports it. Of course I have an understandable preference towards my species and its welfare over many others—for example; smallpox—and within the species I have an understandable preference towards me. I'm certain, as well, that if the Chinook salmon and the Spotted Owl could speak, they'd inform me that they feel the same way. But this preference does not preclude the fact that I have a vested interest in the protection of a sphere greater than my own—that the health of the ecosystem contributes to my health—and if it suffers, so will I.

So then, with a return to sailing, I desire to live a lifestyle of skill: to live in integrity, character; not requiring much in terms of material maintenance or possessions save what directly contributes to my personal health <u>and not a step beyond.</u> Sailing, in its true form, expresses that. The scale of my consumption is a measure of my skill, and even more so, my more lightly encumbered boat sails further and faster. I want to be symbiotic in my relationships rather than parasitic—I do not wish to engage in violence unless it is necessary and constructive. I think that many of those who sail feel this way. As follows, the ecological stance of the true sailor is often cautious and measured but **<u>intense.</u>** We who sail have made the business of the wind, weather, and water our environment—we have a vested interest in its health and stability. We have a vested interest in it that is proportional, again, *to our level of investment.*

Sailing. I think it reflects poorly on the quality of "sailor" one sees in the glossy magazines who requires so much to keep his soft body so comfy and dry as he superficially dabbles about the world. Sincerely, I'm not impressed—though I've (unfairly) been accused of sour grapes at times. Rather than he sailors are always impressed with the fellow who does the most with the least—it is HE that we want to call ship-mate—it is he who is the most elevated example of what we'd like to—and will NEED to—become as the world changes. "Right Living": Livings as light and honestly as possible—this is critical and necessary to the existence of a sailor...

Character. One might rightly forgive a fool for his errors. But a sailor, even an inferior one, even a motorsailor, <u>must</u> be more aware of his world and that which he shares it with than is common. His eyes must always be on the water and the skies—he must know them; his heart must be gladdened to see the porpoises run under his keel. He must feel a camaraderie with the natural world that is seldom seen by those who spend all their time ashore. While one might forgive a fool, it is difficult to forgive a man who will anchor tucked close to shore in a pristine harbor and pump oil impregnated water overboard in order to run his refrigerator. It is hard to forgive the noisy outboard as he fiddles about. It is hard to forgive the—in many cases—obnoxious display of affluence that is involved, a display that is admired by most of the world <u>entirely as much as a kick in the teeth</u>—it is hard to appreciate the necessary track of exploitation that was required to get him there. A sailor has no excuses—a sailor, with a centuries old tradition of being a citizen of the world—should know better. When this display is coupled with the typical profile handed to us by the marketing folks—the half-million dollar yacht, the 100,000 dollar a year lifestyle, the millions of dollars of assets invested in the income generating industrial complex stocks; <u>*yes, at this point I do feel anger and sour grapes*</u>, for those people who had such a large hand in killing the coral reefs <u>also</u> got to see and enjoy them before they died. Unless I hurry, I never will. I never will...

So how to respond? Justice, I will admit, is a metaphysical preference as unjustifiable as any other. I will still insist that the sort of behavior that many of we western sorts engage in certainly does no one any good. I believe quite fundamentally that the environment creates us as much or more than we create it—and what sort of "us" does a world without coral reefs, without panda bears, without *barn swallows* even—imagine; create? I cannot help but believe we will be diminished. Who cares but us—*but we will*. We certainly will...

Boats are not good for the environment. Even an engineless sailboat has toxic bottom paint on the bottom of it. Again, I must admit, however, that *I personally* am not good for the environment at large either. Everything that lives pollutes to some degree. Short of the only environmentally friendly action—suicide—an attuned individual who values that which is valuable makes as small a wake as possible in their passage through life. Engineless boats are far less toxic than powered ones. Small ones less toxic than large. Fiberglass less toxic than wood. Most importantly, the *skills and the lifestyle* that comes from cruising in a small, engineless sailboat is perhaps as ecologically benevolent as one can find. We are on the verge of technology now that may even make heavy–metal based paints unnecessary—which would make a small, engineless, fiberglass sailboat the most efficient and low–impact means of travel in the world—superceding even foot travel which at least lives a print...One cannot help but feel good about this if one has one's eyes open...

These reasons are why I sail. They are not convincing to everyone—however that does not mean that they are not valid. Many people are not up to the task, nor aware enough to value the difference. Still, in spite of what it might look like at this point, I am not here to evangelize: I am here to teach. I sincerely hope that others will find in this the encouragement and the ability to set sail in their smart little craft and be successful and fulfilled in their personal quests.

What is a Sailboat?

A sailboat is a boat that travels from place to place using wind as propulsion. A boat that uses propulsion other than sail is not a sailboat.

Again, it really makes very little sense in comparing sailboats to motorsailers. We will engage in this exercise and make some interesting points, but the truth is that sailboats and motorsailers are funda-mentally different, requiring such different means of handling and having such different concerns that the comparison is nearly useless. Yet to demonstrate the uselessness of this comparison is indeed useful; thus we continue.

I will begin with the most significant yet little known difference between sailboats and motorsailors: Sailing performance. Sailboats are so seldom seen anymore, except as straight racers, that the superior per-formance of their greatly reduced drag and much better ballast ratio has largely been forgotten. Taking a 30 foot boat as an example, an inboard engine and its related gear translates many times into nearly a thousand pounds—or between 10 and 15 percent of displace-ment—the removal meaning perhaps two inches of immersion on a 30 foot boat and *lowering one's effective ballast by several inches!!* How much difference? An engineless boat will typically be a knot to a knot and a half faster than its encumbered twin, and point 5 to 8 degrees higher. It will likely be able to more effective canvas in the same speed of air, and make much better time. The removal of the propeller, shaft and strut—the removal of the propeller aperture as well—*can often cut the total drag of the hull through the water at any given speed fully in half!!* This is terribly significant in the real world, as it makes passages and maneuvers possible that the engine burdened craft could not even con-sider under sail. In many ways then the motorsailor pays a double price—for having the engine means that one needs it more often.

Engines aboard motorsailors are often referred to as safety gear, or something that exists "to get a guy out of a pinch." What is this pinch? A difficult, inconvenient set of circumstances most often gotten into by errors in judgement or incompetence. As I write this, I suppose that I am in a bit of a pinch, I am not in the happy slip that I intended—I am tied to a pier four miles away and I intend to spend the night here. Why? Went sailing today, wind was predicted to be high; it was a bit higher than anticipated and lasted longer than both anticipated and predicted. I felt that the harbor entrance with a four–foot following sea and highly erratic 30 knot winds to be unsafe—so I am elsewhere. Had a fine day of sailing anyway, although a bit wet and cold; I'll have an early wake–up sailing back in the rain and the light winds of the morning. This is a bit inconvenient, I admit it wholeheartedly, but pleasantly so and I have the time to be inconvenienced. Dangerous? Not at all. I knew what I was up against. I knew there was a realistic chance that I would end up where I am. What would be dangerous would be to have attempted the harbor entry; and that factor has nothing to do with the boat, it is completely dependent on me. What IS dangerous, however, is not recognizing the hazards of such an entry, or attempting it with unsuitable means. The engine, if I had one, most likely would have solved the problem for me today, admittedly, but if it had failed in the attempt the result would have been tragic. Modern diesel engines are remarkably reliable, I admit, but they give no warning of failure at all when it occurs, in most cases. As so, reliance on them is not prudence, nor confidence, it is pure blind faith—faith is NOT a virtue at sea. If one wants to see a proverbial "pinch" look at the kinds of situations relying on engines can get you into. Sail, for all its virtues, isn't likely to get you out of the worst of these.

It is difficult to claim something as in the interest of "safety" that is more likely to cause a dangerous mishap than less. One must be more cautious and sure under sail, and because of that fact sailboats seldom find themselves in the "pinch." Well–designed sailboats are very handy under sail and it is rare that the boat can be blamed for accidents. Being on the water without appropriate skill is certainly not safe—engines mask that lack of skill until problems arise—can something that masks danger and removes none of it really be considered a safety device?

Most boating related injuries are *machinery* related.

Many modern boats designed as motorsailors have been designed under the assumption that the motor is operational and used. Even the sailing rigs show that. If one must set sail under sail one needs gear capable of that. Things like full batten mains and roller–furling, both of which expect a boat to be brought to weather under power to set, reef and stow, are useless and dangerous. So are radically swept spreaders and other non–utilitarian effects—these are of no use to a sailor. Most of that gear simply gets in the way—it is another thing to foul. Sailing demands hulls that are balanced and rigs that are balanced, frankly sacrificing the top ten percent of performance in highly unusual conditions to gain the bottom ninety percent in all conditions. True sailing vessels are ALWAYS performance vessels—regardless of their form. Perform they must. Extra weight is dead weight.

Types of Sailboats Suitable for Voyaging under Sail:

Most people when they think of engineless cruising think of purists aboard gaff–rigged pilot cutters, Ingrids, and the like. Heavy cruisers are indeed popular as motorsailors but uncommon among sailors. Why? Most of these vessels were designed as working craft and with the intent of carrying great amounts of stuff—also popular among the motorized cruising set—and their rigs and sail–plans reflected that in their day. The working canvas of a true pilot cutter would likely be double what passes as a pilot cutter today—sailing them was difficult, strenuous, and tiring work. They were certainly not designed as pleasure craft. The best of them, rigged properly, made remarkable way to weather (though not by modern standards) but it was a wet and rugged ride. Contrary to the popular myth, most pound hard on the wind, ride rough in a seaway, roll ponderously, and are fearsomely hard on their own gear. They are also mightily expensive to keep up. As a working boat, with hired crew, none of this is objectionable. For a small crew interested in a pleasant time, however, it is often a bit much. Those who sell the modern versions of the boats know this and keep the sail–plans very modest—too much so to really expect to make way in most condition—so the work of sailing this style of boats is kept manageable. As engineless boats—with a strong crew and a gale, many of them will keep themselves off a lee shore—but driving them hard will exhaust a small crew in short order. For many applications, most even, I see them as unacceptable craft.

People will argue—including some people that I have a great deal of respect for—who HAVE sailed the world in the gaff-rigged pilot cutter. Sure, I will not argue with results. A great deal of the matter is preference—how one likes to sail and where one likes to sail—if one really likes gaff-rigged pilot cutters then that is fine. My point is this—for me, and I think for most people, they are going to get a great deal more pleasure out of a folkboat, for example, then they might that pilot cutter. Before they are concerned with sailing to New Zealand they should be concerned with sailing their local bay. In either case, those with a folkboat are going to go more places with less effort, less expense, faster and simpler. I don't really think there is a sensible debate about that. You can, for certain, carry more gear in the pilot cutter than in the folkboat—but I personally don't see the wisdom in carrying a good deal of gear to begin with. Sailing a folkboat is MUCH less work. A folkboat, as an example again, is a more efficient sailing vessel. For most people, I think a folkboat would make much more sense.

A very common misconception—used as an argument for large heavy craft—is involved the effect of displacement on seakindliness. There is a relationship, but not what is typically stated. In a true sea, where ride matters, any boat much under two hundred tons is tossed pretty badly. Comparing 28 foot light displacement boats to 50 foot heavy displacement boats is not a significant as many would think. In comparably mild conditions, however, the ride for the small boat gets busy quicker, this is certain. It is also buttoned down and ready for a blow in next to no time, while the larger boat is much more of an exercise. It is doubly difficult on a rolling deck when the work is heavy enough to demand *both hands*. I personally feel that the ride of a moderate small boat to be far more comfortable that of the heavier vessel—the motion may be quicker at times, but less "powerfully ponderous." This sensation has to be felt to be described; my point is to insert a word of caution.

On to the other end of the spectrum: racing boats. One might think that in light of the previous argument, there is something to be said for a race boat as a cruiser. Indeed there is—especially an engineless boat—as long as the hull form is not radical enough to produce handling idiosyncrasies. This eliminates many of the most modern racers from consideration—most are simply too squirrelly to handle short-handed. Unfortunately most of them are also built too light to handle the wear and tear a true boat suffers. Still, I have met sailors cruising on fairly radical race boats, single-handed and engineless—something I can seldom say for the heavy boats. One fellow, in particular stands out—an excellent sailor—and was willing to live with the very rigid demands of keeping his boat light and sailing it in race trim everywhere he went. Most sailors are not so disciplined nor as vigorous as he; I am personally willing to sacrifice a degree of pointing for the ability to carry an extra case of beer. I am not willing to sacrifice 3 degrees—but 1 degree I will: This is really all one gains by going with a radical boat as opposed to one that is simply well proportioned and sailed well.

In the mid 1960's and early 1970's a type of boat was developed called the cruiser/racer. There were a number of boats designed and manufactured that are of this type. Carl Alberg, William Shaw, Olin Stephens; these are representative designers of this type of boat. Each had particular signature styles but one thing in common: balance. The hulls were balanced, the interiors modest, the ballast ratios excellent, the rigs moderate in aspect. Many of these boats are extremely handy and fast sailors—in my mind representing close to an ideal—the most boat one can get without sacrificing any one characteristic. Many of these boats reflect the bias of an era in which the engine truly WAS an auxiliary, and ARE capable of functioning in absence of it—seldom seen today. Few boats of this type are manufactured today—I would advise buying an original—start with the Pearson Triton as a paradigm and develop one's preference from there. I sail a Pearson "Renegade" if you care about my preference.

Shall I describe the ideal sailboat for single–handing, as I see it? In my mind, for a single handing sailor an ideal boat would be 28 feet overall, 8 $^1/_2$ feet abeam with a symmetrical waterline that ends up being about 22 feet on the water in cruising trim. I'd expect the boat to weigh about 6800 pounds light, I'd expect to draw about 4 feet. At least 2300 pounds of that should be lead in an encapsulated keel. A well sprung and low sheerline. I'd like to see a fairly good sized underbody—preferably a modified full keel with a cut away forefoot and a balanced spade rudder. Not quite wineglass but close, with a nearly flat run at the boats optimum angle of heel. A large rudder as well, much larger than is fashionable. The masthead rig will be balanced to this hull, with nearly half–beam spreaders and about a height of 32 feet off the total deadrise. Relatively large main—capable of sailing under a reefed main alone or trysail in heavy air. Am I not describing a beautiful boat? Of course—but one not built except in custom yards. Why? One is only going to get about 5 feet, 10 inches of headroom out of this hull, and the interior living space will be about half of that of a typical boat show 28 foot boat. Besides, this will be an expensive boat to build, and there is practically no market for quality boats in this type and size range. Marketing has won…

How to Sail:

N ow it becomes obvious that much is and has been said about sailing. A look through the bookshelves of any bookstore will demonstrate this fact. Our goal here is not to add to the pile of data, nor to
provoke debate, but to rather preface the context so we can speak of
sailing with our peculiar attitude—not of theory, but of practice.

I faced a bit of an ethical dilemma when being asked to write this
book. There are, again, a lot of books out there about "sailing." I'm
trying to do something a bit different—perhaps rather than compile a
list of dum–dum skills, maybe to communicate an *attitude that carries
the necessity of certain skills with it.* People have a funny idea about they
learn things, and generally an over–estimated idea of how they do so. I
remember a time back when I was in college when a "friend" I had
came to me with a question. Now to preface let me say this was the sort
of guy who was Mensa member but everybody else thought was an
idiot…he said that he had a date with a girl the coming Friday. He
asked me if I'd teach him how to play the guitar. Now I was shocked,
of course, as much by the request as by the fact that he had a date, but
it illustrated a point very clearly. Playing a guitar is just a matter of
knowing chords, right? Learn a couple of chords and that's really all
there is to it. Learning Aikido is just a matter of learning a couple of
moves, right? Learning sailing is just a matter of learning to tack, jibe,
and scream "Ready About!"…

There is no substitute for spending time on the water. I could tell
you how to sail in and out of a slip in great detail a thousand
times—this will do nothing but warm armchairs. If I can convince you
that you CAN actually do such a thing, and should, and effectively
enough that you do so—then you'll learn to sail with no help from me

at all. So then, I try to convey the need, and to point at things that one should certainly know, with the hope that the reader will take the message to heart...

So much of learning is realizing what one does not know, and what one must then learn...

Sailing, kernalized, is simple. It is simply motion—hopefully forward—generated by the forces of wind. Controlled sailing is the act of balancing all the forces acting upon a boat—not just wind but the forces that come from the boat itself moving through the water—both simple hydrodynamic lift as well as wave action. All forces acting upon the boat in total contribute to the boat's course and speed.

The most difficult and interesting case to explain—as well the most important—is the case of a boat sailing to weather. This is the case where wind blows across sails rather than to into them, where lift is generated rather than drag, and where the balance of all forces acting upon a boat become most critical and important. This is where we begin our conversation.

Basically, of course, when a wind stream encounters an object, it separates and flows around it, re–connecting with itself on the downwind side at some distances and after generating a good deal of turbulence. If the shape happens to be an wing, basically meaning any asymmetrical shape where the flow on one side of the object must travel a greater distance than the airflow on the other side—lift is generated. This lift is simply a conservation of energy issue—Bernoulli's principle of high speed creating low pressure, low speed creating high pressure—thus the greater distance side requires a higher speed of the airflow, thus lower pressure, thus "suction," thus lift in that direction.

A relatively simple concept. The difficulty is that the amount of lift generated has a direct impact on the speed of the boat, and of course, due to the nature of "apparent wind," the speed of the boat has a direct impact on the amount of lift generated. The velocity made good to weather is the quantity we seek, and this is dependent on a great number of variables.

Thus sailing, again, simple in theory, difficult in practice. Many problems arise in application that detract from the efficiency of this windward lift. First off, the sail is not a rigid object, and the shape of it itself is determined by a certain angle of attack to the airflow—likely less than ideal—which is required to keep the sail set. The sail has irregularities to it, and a surface that has some amount of friction to it, which causes turbulence and interrupted airflow, again destroying lift. The speed and density of the air itself is hardly constant, nor is it often a true laminar airflow—thus turbulence is introduced even before wind meets sail. The angle of attack of the sail to the wind, at least in any sort of seaway, is not constant either, and thus the sail must be oriented for "optimum" drive, not "ideal" efficiency. Thus a good deal of guesswork is involved—theory can be a effective guess, but it is still a guess, and the main trick to sailing any boat well, is to learn the boat and find what peculiar combination of sail and orientation is best.

Still there are certainly issues which are relatively constant. Sailing closer to the wind gets us up wind quicker than sailing further off the wind. Sailing on the wind, sails are trimmed, more or less, as inboard as possible without inducing stall. Stall? Stall occurs when the angle of attack to the airflow is too great, and the airstream on the high–speed side is in essence flung off the sail due to sheer inertia—resulting in turbulence and loss of drive. This occurs near the section of the sail with maximum camber, as one might expect, as here the centripetal acceleration is the greatest. Stall occurs quite often in sails, but its effect is often invisible and only shows up as reduced speed. Yet much can be learned by studying stall. Though not we're not going into these in great detail, we will address the issue. A sailor in a pure sailing craft has a need for speed—he is always in a race against the elements—he races both with and against the tide, the wind, with storms and calms. There are good reference texts on this material if further study is desired. Rather than reading, however, I will always recommend sailing...

Complications to think about at some point: a digression.

High aspect airfoils are more prone to stall than low aspect airfoils from change in angle of incidence in airflow. Thus high aspect airfoils, though hypothetically more efficient, require more control of angle of attack to retain that efficiency.

Cold wet air is denser than hot dry air, and has much greater inertia. Thus is far more likely to break away from the sail, although it also generates more lift.

A full cut sail with a good deal of camber to it, though it generates more powerful lift, generates more centripetal acceleration and thus stalls sooner, generating potentially less lift, especially at speed. It certainly creates a good deal more drag and thus heel.

Flat sails stall less quickly, though they generate less lift. Still they are capable of carrying that lift to higher speed potential.

Flat sails are more closewinded than full, though they accelerate less quickly and may then generate a good deal of lee–way on some designs of hull before they get to speed.

The draft position of a sail has an effect on stall and lift as well. If the draft position is well forward, the sail stalls less easily and sets more readily, but generates proportionally less lift. If the draft is well aft, more of the sail generates lift but the sail overall is more prone to stall.

The slot effect: The interaction of the headsail and the mainsail. This is all critical and seldom understood. The purpose of the slot effect is not so much to speed up the air over the main, although it does this too, but as much as the trailing air off the inside of the headsail is redirected towards the after part of the main and prevents stall on the mainsail. Thus the sum effect of the two together is much greater than the two apart. How effective this re attachment of airflow can be is complicated by a number of factors—how deep the overlap of the headsail is relative to the main; how wide the slot is, whether the twist of the two match, whether the leech shapes match—but now we are getting into the art of trimming a sail for going to weather.

The point?: That it isn't as simple as things might seem. One hears, especially from people who sell boats and boat products, that one thing is good, and another bad—etc. Again, it isn't nearly so simple. If one wants to design a sail, or a boat for that matter, that only does one thing—like sail around three yellow things in a bay on later summer afternoons, on flat water, and under 12 knots of air—it is a relatively simple matter to maximize for that scenario. But this is not the kind of sailing we are talking about in this book. We desire a boat, and sails, that operate at the highest level of efficiency over the broadest range of possible conditions. What kind of boat or sail is that? Well, that remains to be seen…I say this to temper the hype.

On to the practical.

Starting with the basic trim of the mainsail, there are in essence two things to watch for. The first is the amount the sail is sheeted in relative to the centerline of the boat, and the second is how much twist is in the sail. These are very much the same issue—if a sail has a great deal of twist it really means your are only sheeting in and using the bottom of it. If a sail has very little twist it means we are using most or all of it. Very interrelated concepts, but we will deal with them separately for purposes of explanation.

Setting up for a weather course, close hauled, if we were new to a boat we might sheet the main sheet in fully inboard, amidships, and then slowly ease the mainsheet until the luff of the mainsail just starts to flutter, and then we harden it up again out just so it stops. This is the starting position, and relatively close to where the sail should be for a weather course. The problem is twist. When a mainsail suffers from twist, the result is that the head falls off to leeward and will then lift and luff faster than the rest of the sail. If this is corrected merely by sheeting the boom further inward, the bottom of the sail will be too far sheeted inboard for its own good and will stall too early. The key is some sort of vang or kicking strap which pulls the boom down, rather than in, and thus tightens the leech. Tightening the leech hauls the top of the sail inward in relation to the lower part of the sail, this allows the boom to be eased and thus much higher efficiency to be found throughout the sail.

Yet we can have too much of a good thing. If we tighten the leech excessively by too much downward pull—the leech becomes so tight that it hooks to weather. This makes the draft of the sail fuller, as the sail is more cup shaped now. This, as we've seen, might be good or bad. It might be good because a fuller sail is a more powerful sail and generates more lift. It also generates more heel. It also generates less speed—as the full shape retards airflow more—of course this is where we got our lift. So basically, for sailing in flat water—a cupped shape is likely not such a good idea, a flat shape makes more sense as the drag on the hull is at a minimum. In high winds, it doesn't make much sense either, as we are likely already fighting with heel and weather helm. In tight quarters handling, perhaps for tacking through a marina, the cup might be good, or might not—the cupped sail likely does not point as high as the flat one, but the cupped sail will generate drive more quickly and will be more responsive. So what does a person do? Learn to sail one's boat. Understand what makes an effect happen.

And yes, it may not be quite so simple yet. If the vang pulls down so that the entire boom comes down as a unit, with no bend, the tension in the sail will be primarily translated the leech, as we've said. But if the vanging action comes down into the middle of the boom, and the boom bends, a good deal of tension will be applied to the middle of the sail as well, flattening it as a unit. All the effects we've spoken of apply. Thus, the use of the vang isn't dogma either.

Knowing this, if one has a mainsheet that leads to the end of the boom—as many boats have—and a kicking strap on a boom–horseshoe that can be moved fore and aft and set up in a number of configurations, we can control things very readily if we understand what the effects will be.

So then, hauling a sail in trims it. Hauling it down removes twist. Depending on where the downward pressure is applied will have an effect on whether the sail is made more full or flattened by the action of the vang.

A mainsheet traveler, of course does basically both of these functions in one, although a vang or a kickingstrap is significantly more powerful and versatile, as we have said. On smooth water and light air in most boats it makes sense to have the traveler well to weather. Yes, this tending angle on the boom allows twist and will cause the boom and lower part of the sail to be somewhat oversheeted. This is true, but as the wind is light twist will not be extreme, the narrow entry will allow one to point higher, the slight hook to windward generated at the bottom of the sail is generally offset by greater speed to weather. As the wind speed increases, the effect of drag and stall will be felt, mostly through increased weather helm. Twist will increase, the boom will need to be eased and vang tension applied, or the traveler moved to leeward to counteract this effect. As wind speed increases further, a certain amount of twist can be allowed into the sail to feather the top and to diminish heel, at this one should be considering a reef but sometimes this isn't practical or the increased wind is perhaps local and temporary—at any rate the amount of drive from the bottom half of a large sail is different than the drive from the total of a reefed sail, though how so is dependant on the boat. Again, one will have to sail one's boat to determine which is most effective. The issue becomes pointed when there is a bit of a lumpy sea, the boat will be moving slower than it would be in smooth water—more power is demanded out of the sails rather than speed, a reefed sail which likely will be flatter and can be trimmed free of twist is often the best solution at this point.

Also, it can be noted that twist can flatten a sail. How so? Because one should note that the air flow moves across the sail in a straight line—if one eyes this straight line one will see that in a sail that has a good deal of twist, the middle section of the sail is often quite flat and free of much draft. Is this good or bad? Depends on the sail. At any rate, if the sail has twist, to some degree the head and foot are not at optimum angles to the wind. We've discussed this. Yet perhaps if we sacrifice the head—which does little anyway, and the foot, which may be running in a great deal of turbulence, to optimize the middle—we may make a advantageous gain in *total* lift. Indeed, much of the time this is the case in heavy air. All the time? No. Depends a great deal on the boat, how it is sailed, and the conditions. Again, I will not tell you what is right, only to look for a possibility…

As for headsails, the situation is much the same but the solution is different. The issue again is how far sheeted in and how much twist. The control is different, as the question is how much sheet tension and how far forward or aft will be the sheet car lead? If one moves the car forward, obviously more tension is applied to the leech than the foot, and twist is removed—again powering up the sail. If the sheet car is moved aft, the leech is allowed to rise and more twist develops. How much is ideal? Depends on the boat and the sail. Again, in light air and flat water, the headsail is often trimmed for a leech closed by having the car well forward and the sheet thus further eased. As the wind builds, the sail gets the car moves aft until good shape can no longer be controlled, the top of the sail begins to fall off and helm balance becomes poor. At this point we are looking at a headsail change, and the whole process begins again.

How balanced is the helm? Any more than about 5 degrees of rudder is likely starting to slow the boat down…does it make sense then to carry the imbalance in the sails? It depends—some boats drive very well overcanvased and with atrocious weather helm—especially many older race boats of the 1940's and 1950's. Modern boats want to run more upright and the presence of a good deal of weather helm is often a problem. The only way to know is to make the change and observe the change in speed. Still, more than 5 degrees of rudder is a good place to start thinking about the issue.

The key to the slot effect between the headsail and the main is this: First, to make sure that the headsail is sheeted properly and then the main is sheeted to match. Since the mainsail is to some degree running in air off of the headsail this is the prudent way to go about it for many boats. Secondly, it is important to make sure that the headsail is not oversheeted as in relation to the main as this will choke the slot, and the airflow redirected off the headsail will blow directly into the main, sometimes driving it inside out with the appearance of luffing. This is not luffing however, although the appearance can easily confuse a beginner. This effect can also be caused by too much leech tension in the headsail—as we might expect. Just like in the main, if we apply too much tension to the leech, the headsail becomes cupped—if it is too cupped it drives air directly into the lee side of the main. Experiment to know what is correct—correct simply means fast. Last, it is important to match the twist in the headsail and the main so that the slot effect works from the bottom of the main to the top, not just one place or another. This can be seen well from sighting up behind the mainsail and looking for a uniform camber. It is certainly readily apparent from other boats—and a little radio contact can be useful if one has a sailing friend who will play tag and watch for trim. Again, there is theory and there is practice—again, we are looking for the optimum, not the ideal—and what that may be on any given boat may be a bit of a surprise.

The last thing to consider—position of the draft in headsail or main. This is controlled basically by halyard tension. As wind speed increases, cloth stretches, the sail bellies, and the point of maximum camber moves aft. This causes the vector of lift to move aft as well, causing more heel and less lift. The stretch from the cloth can be removed to some degree by increasing the halyard tension, thus again pulling the bellied cloth up and down rather than aft. It is important to know how cloth stretches—as it is an important clue to how sails work. When a sail stretches, at least in a modern sail, very little of the change in shape comes from actual elongation of the fibers in the cloth. Most of the stretch comes along the bias of the sail, as the lay of the cloth changes shape. Thus, the application of halyard tension more than anything balances the pressure of the wind and pulls the shape of the cloth back into its original form. If, for example, the lay of the cloth makes for little diamond shapes between the weave—the force of the wind likely stretches this diamond shape side to side and flattens the diamond—thus the sail bellies. If we apply halyard tension to the top and bottom of this diamond, it is pulled back into its original shape, and the sail into the shape it was cut to have. As a rule of thumb, the halyard tension need only be tight enough to pull the sag out of the sail at any given wind speed. Thus in light air, only enough tension to remove the wrinkles is necessary—in heavy air, however a bit of Norwegian Steam might be called for.

Sag in the headstay or bend in the mast to leeward also cause a sail to belly and move aft, causing weather helm problems. This is an issue solved by proper rig tune and tension. A significant issue, it has a significant effect on boat speed—and is more complicated than one might think—there is a section on this issue located later in this book.

This is sailing to weather close hauled. Sailing on all other weather points of sail are in essence the same, but the interaction of slot becomes less pronounced, and to a good degree the control of twist becomes more. Still the principles remain exactly the same as long as wind is blowing across sails and not into them.

Sailing downwind is purely about wind blowing into sails. It is about generating drag. The key to speed and efficiency off the wind is dependent primarily on how much canvas one can carry—pure square footage. It is also controlled to a certain extent by helm balance, as some extreme sail combinations may cause such weather helm that speed is diminished—that is, just before a broach.

Of course there are tricks and techniques…the one I would suggest is that in sloop rigged boats there are seldom many good reasons to run directly dead down wind, wing and wing. There are many that view this a some sort of stunt of helmsmanship, and to some degree it is as it requires more attention and provides less feedback than any other point of sail. Yet in many conditions, it is an ineffective means to sail, and if there is any sea state, uncomfortable as well. It depends on the boat, and depends on the conditions, of course, but in many cases running broad is a faster course or at least no slower in terms of speed of advance than running dead down, the course itself is certain to be a more comfortable one, and sheet to tiller steering gear works very well—which it does not for a wing and wing course. At any rate, and on any course down wind, the key is to avoid a gibe—this is much easier to do if running broad than running dead down as well. Using a boom preventer is good practice, and at any rate can be used to vang the boom down, preventing chafe as well as flattening the sail and providing more area, but a gibe with a boom preventer still runs an appreciable chance of tearing a mainsail, and by no means calls for less attention at the helm.

Watch for chafe when sailing down wind. On most boat it is very likely that the main sail will chafe on the shrouds to some degree—make sure these surfaces are smooth. Again, vang the boom down acting as a gibe preventer as well as diminishing chafe.

Realize that in any kind of sea–way, a small boat will often roll badly sailing dead down wind. The beamier the boat is, generally the more pronounced this is. For this reason I almost never sail dead down wind, greatly preferring to tack back and forth Again, the zigzag course seldom makes for any difference in the speed of advance because the course is sailed at a considerably higher speed—but in light conditions one may as well sail the most direct course and be done with it. Of course, at these times, roll is not an issue.

Many people have come to enjoy sailing down wind under a large headsail alone. Traditionally called "scudding," there is nothing new about it nor is there is anything wrong with this technique as long as the sail is built to withstand the strain. Unfortunately, it seldom is. Especially when the headsail is a roller–furling type, designed to carry and set in relatively light air, the act of carrying it full or partly rolled in any kind of wind is almost certain to ruin it in short order. Beware of this.

Now on to even more practical matters—how to handle sail on a sailing boat, without the aid of crew or engine. Suppose one is sailing on one's way towards the islands and needs to make a headsail change? How is this done without the aid of a helmsman or an auto pilot?

Most boats will have a natural course to weather that they will steer with—nearly close–hauled and with the tiller lashed. We will get into this in great deal in a little bit—but for now a short explanation of why will suffice. When wind hits a sail it generates heel and lift. The heel, of course, is directed sideways rather than forward, and depending if the sail is up forward in the boat or aft in the boat, this sideways motion will tend to push either the stern of the boat downwind, or the bow down wind. This much is simple. The more important effect is this—lift. As lift is generated, it pulls the boat forward. But because heel is occurring, and because the sail then is not on the centerline of the boat, the area from which the forward drive is located is not on the centerline of the boat either. Thus lift causes a boat to want to turn to weather as well, and in direct proportion to its strength.

Most boats can take advantage of this to create a course equilibrium to weather. Generally speaking, the boom is let out a bit low of a close hauled course and the tiller is lashed slightly to weather to keep the helm down. The key is to find an equilibrium where the boat is pinching and luffing, and slowing working to weather. Most of the time this will be a stable enough course for a single–handed sailor to go forward and make a headsail change. Of course, in this case, the headsail is let flog, the main is appropriately sheeted, the tiller lashed, and the head-sail change is made, in that order.

The reason this works is simple but a bit difficult to understand. The reason it works is this: if a boat is sailing and it for some reason falls off the wind a bit it will heel more—because the sails are now trimmed less efficiently. The sails are now too much sheeted in, are stalling, and generating very little drive, the boat slows and the predominant forces left are all acting to turn the boat to weather. If the boat turns to weather, the boat heels a little less, the slight application of rudder becomes predominant, and the boat falls off the wind. Somewhere in here is an equilibrium where the boat steers a steady course. Don't expect it to cross oceans, but the course will be stable enough to get a headsail change done.

If one has learned the tricks of sheet to tiller steering, a sheet to tiller gear set up off the main sheet will perform this task even better and allow some distance to be made effectively as the headsail change is occurring. That discussion is forthcoming.

As for the task of putting in a reef, single–handed—this can be more of a scramble. Again the technique will depend a bit on the boat. Some boats under a close sheeted headsail and a lashed helm will hold a course much like they might under the main, other boats are very unstable under these circumstances and do not cooperate at all. Again, one will have to experiment. Sheet to tiller gear is of little use here as well, as the only sheet that can be used is the jib sheet, and this seldom seems to be effective without the interaction of the main. Still, in many cases a combination can be found of reasonable stability under a headsail alone where the boat naturally steers a close reach, which allows the boom to be sheeted out and at least enough time—perhaps with an occasional scramble back to the helm—to get a reef put in. The key, as in all these things is practiced hands operating with efficiency—there is no reason why a mainsail cannot be reefed on a small boat in a matter of seconds—assuming one is proficient. This proficiency can be tested at the dock, and should be, by attempting to put a reef in, blindfolded, with a group of buddies howling and throwing buckets of water. This exercise is simple compared to putting a reef in at sea, for the boat isn't pitching, yet it will certainly make one aware quickly of what problems are likely to present themselves.

Many older texts suggest heaving–to for sail evolutions. I do not think many modern boats have the proper balance or underbodies to do so readily. My boat, hove–to, still fore–reaches at an appreciable speed no matter what I do. This is not necessarily a problem, and makes for a quick trick when making a sandwich, but I do not see the technique as being useful for sail changes. Better, I think, is plan to make way and to continue to make way. We have described how to do so.

We can also see that if we are sailing a boat, and not motorsailing, how much more we rely on our sails. On a motorsailing boat, or indeed many boats, the first reef that is taken is the furling of the head-sail—which many times is a roller–furling unit. This is well and convenient, but would make the task of reefing a main much more difficult if the engine wasn't in use, as there would be no drive to keep course stability while the reef is being tucked in—and the only alternative is to lie a–hull and roll badly. This is certainly not the best seamanship nor the best conditions to tie in a tidy reef.

I personally do not see either roller–furling units nor full–batten mains as appropriate gear aboard a sailboat. There are certainly advantages of convenience to each, but the fact remains that on a sailboat one hasn't the luxury of motoring to weather to make sail changes. To large a large degree both full–batten mains and roller–furling demand this—there are times which it can become necessary to reef a mainsail that is partially drawing, while sailing downwind. I am doubtful this could be done to a full batten sail without damaging it, or having the cars jam, or some other catastrophe. I haven't the final word on this, some disagree, but be certain one considers the issues and the potential ramifications of each carefully.

VANG THE BOOM DOWN SECURELY when tying in a reef, it makes the project much more simple and gives a sailor something to hold onto as one works.

These problems in headsail changes and in reefing are typical—one finds stiff piston hanks that haven't been maintained—and in the wet and cold of a pitching foredeck can be insurmountable. One can find that the slide gate on the mast is frozen as well—this can be cata-strophic. One can certainly discover that one can be afflicted with dyslexia involving a simple reef knot, yet the reef knot must be applied exactly the same and with a protocol—I suggest always tied with one side slipped, the slip loop pointing up. If that moment occurs when a reef then needs to be taken OUT in the dark, it makes the job much simpler. There is very little as frustrating with having to deal with a mystery knot in the dark with frozen fingers. One is tempted to apply a knife, and this is often the only resort, but a poor solution this is…

And yes, a sailor always carries a knife, and yes, a knife with a point on it has no place aboard a boat. This was a safety issue 300 years ago, and the same issue remains. An edge is much less likely to inflict random damage than a point.

While we are on the subject of safety issues, I'll need to make a position clear. Safety gear is reasonable, so far as it goes, as long as one never makes the mistake of using it. Safety gear more often than not is found to be relied upon, and as such I see it as creating hazards of its own. Lifelines are perhaps a good example. Rare is the boat that has lifelines that would seriously be capable of keeping a full grown man aboard in a seaway. Putting an extra piece of string or netting on them solves nothing. It would be little effort to grab the typical life line stanchion and simply bodily tear it off a boat—they are simply not strong enough to be effective. They could be built that strong, I suppose, but on a small boat the heft of the hardware would be excessive. Not to suggest taking lifelines off a boat, necessarily, as their real purpose is to keep a slightly tipsy sailor on board his boat while in an anchorage, but also not to suggest that they are really any more than ornament as a piece of safety gear. The only solution for a small boat is a set of proper jackstays and with the crew in harnesses. Floatation aids, man–overboard markers and the such are only then encumbrance. The thing any sailor and crew should realize that to go over the side of a boat means certain death—some people magically escape, of course, but death indeed is the practical reality of the issue. It is an especially grim issue for the single–hander. When asked of man overboard drills, the Col. Blondie Hasler replied that he simply instructed his crew to drown like a proper English gentleman. I've always though that was the best advice I had ever heard on the subject.

Docking and Close Quarters Boat Handling:

Docking and sail–handling in tight quarters makes a lot of people nervous. This shouldn't be the case, necessarily, but certainly it is the situation which can take a lack of skill—normally hidden in convenience and large amounts of space in which to be sloppy—and makes it apparent. Again, there are not really any good reasons for this attitude. A good sailboat, well handled, is nearly as maneuverable as a car in a parking lot is—many people are nervous sailing ten feet from a pier but not nervous about flying down the freeway sometimes inches from a careening semi–truck. The key, of course, is practice and experience, so the first step again is to get out on the boat and run through some drills in basic boat handling.

People speak of marinas that prohibit sailing inside the breakwater. There are such places, admittedly, but they are certainly few—and I go so far to say that the prohibition of sailing is a good indicator of a lot of unfriendliness and a good place to avoid. Most all the marinas I have encountered were absolutely positive and supportive of good boat handling practices, as well as were other boaters.

I think there is really very little of an excuse here.

I should point out, however, that I'm writing this focusing on moderate sized sailboats—perhaps 24 to 34 feet on deck. A lot of yachtsmen like to say with an indignant snort that their boat is bigger than that and because of that one couldn't possibly sail it in and out of a harbor. This is absolute ignorant bullshit and deserves a bit of a retort. I've seen and personally sailed a 112 foot, 200 ton, square rigged brig in and out of a marina—I think that's likely a bit bigger than any boat we're talking about here. The size of the boat is *not* the key issue.

Anybody who proclaims to know anything about prudent seamanship or boat handling must admit that the primary and most fundamental attribute of a safe, well–handled boat is the ratio of crew strength to boat size—the brig in question had a trained, skilled 14 person crew. One cannot ignore the reality of the importance of crew strength. Bigger boats are not more difficult to sail as engineless craft providing that they are well crewed. In many ways, they are easier to sail. They stand up to a blow better. With their taller rigs, they are less often becalmed. They, being heavier, often achieve a better sail set in light air and a chop. They carry way and steerage further. The only thing more difficult about large boats is this: if one makes an error in boat handling, it is bound to be a large error, and one is bound to smash things in a large way. This can be troublesome, for certain.

Practically speaking, however, it is tough enough to find enough crew skill to handle a Sunfish let alone a Wondrous 50 in tight quarters—when the foredeck bum makes yet another dash to the mast to douse the main—as he fumbles through the halyards to find the correct one yet again—as you're coming dead down into a dock in a blow trying to explain to some dolt yet again what a waist spring line is—you're heading for disaster. Not to say it can't be done, it just probably requires a professional crew. It used to be that the fat cats with big boats knew this—they hired a professional crew to run the boat so the owner and his family and friends could actually sit back and have a good time. People don't have that much taste anymore so the owner just yells and screams at his spouse…

There is no virtue in running shorthanded. It is foolhardy. Unless you can carry all the sail you want, in the conditions you want to, as long as you want to—you've got too much boat on your hands—and you'll not be "sailing" it anywhere.

Part of the reason people want big boats (other than status again) is because bigger boats have more interior space. They do—but not if they're properly crewed. If one compares the practical interior room of a 28 foot boat with a single–hander aboard, to a 50 foot boat with a crew of six—I think one will agree with me that the 28 foot boat feels much more roomy…

Back to boat handling…

I think it is important that one of the way one demonstrates one's superior boat handling skill is to make sure one doesn't inconvenience other boaters in the display of it. What I mean by this is demanding right–of–way, or basically being in the way of other boaters on a mad rush out of the harbor. Other boaters of less skill will certainly be obstructions—just assume that this is part of the game. If one chooses good times to make entries and exits—this is seldom a problem. When the weather is difficult and so is the harbor entry, traffic inside the harbor is invariably light. In these cases, be sure one uses all the proper signals if necessary, and sails with assertion. There is no question that you have a right here, and so do what you will—personally I have never had it become a problem.

Fortunately, most of the time that the sailing is really good, most people are too afraid to go out and the traffic is bound to be light. If one sails the tide rather than the cocktail hour, one will find that traffic is seldom a problem either.

When cruising, it is often very hard to know what lies behind the breakwater. In these cases it is irresponsible to sail in blind—so one must wait for conditions that are appropriate for a very careful approach, even if it means sculling inside in a flat calm—or sending in a dingy to investigate before entering. This may seem like an inconvenience but it is certainly a reasonable part of nautical tradition and practice—one should not feel inconvenienced at all.

Those cautions being raised, there are really only a few scenarios that one can face. Which are getting on and off a dock, or getting in and out of a slip. Practically, getting in and out of a slip is just getting on and off of a very short dock. For practicing these maneuvers, use the longest dock you can find to make the maneuver safe, but mark the dock off in a distance only as long as your slip. That way you learn to only use as much dock space as you need—and this will become critical.

Before you try anything, however, you'll need to know a couple of things about your boat. These are basic skills. First, at any given speed, how far will the boat carry way? Try to think in terms of boat–lengths rather than feet, as you'll always have a ready measuring stick. In other words, if you pull off the sail power, how far will the boat coast and maintain steerage? This varies quite a bit from boat to boat, keels make a difference here, but you need to know your boat very well. Some maneuvers are nothing more than just coasting into place. Learn to judge distance.

Secondly, you'll need to know what the turning radius of your boat is—also think again in terms of boat lengths. For many modern boats with powerful rudders, this is just over one boat length—older designs often require more room. Think, as well, that when one makes a turn that the action of the rudder is going to kill some speed—this can be useful to burn off excess speed or can be an inconvenience. Be aware of the possibilities.

Third, you'll need to know what the boat does when you initially APPLY sail power—some boats take off a little bit before the rudder gains steerage and often in a marina you haven't room for this surprise. Again, all of this can be practiced out in the open with no risk to anything—so take advantage of that possibility before you go and scratch paint.

So go and, put the boat through its paces. What I do when I teach people to sail is this: Take people out and throw a cushion overboard—sail circles around it—the tighter the better. Now, throw a second one over the side, and sail figure eights. Can't do it? Miss any tacks? That is unacceptable. Do this until it becomes positively boring. You need to be as comfortable sailing as you are driving your car—I assume you can drive your car.

After this is easy—which takes most people about an hour—sail up to a cushion, stop, and sail away again. Is this easy? It should be. It will teach you that some approaches make a lot more sense than others. This will teach you low speed control, how far the boat carries way, etc. Some boats are just not very comfortable with low speed handling. This is one of the curses of modern design. Since they design boats for a minimum of wetted surface area and control surface area, the amount of control the boat has is very heavily dependent on its speed. At low speed many of these designs are very difficult to keep under control—take this into consideration if you haven't purchased a boat yet.

After this, you might try moorings someplace. The difference between moorings and the cushions is that you've likely got obstacles to dodge while making your approach—so one learns to make clever approaches and begins to think about locating escape routes. You'll learn quickly that it is always nice to try to make your approaches to weather, if you can, and that down wind approaches are always more difficult and less forgiving.

It is also helpful to find some place where the tide sets through the moorings—and learn a little about relative velocity. Having current present is not as difficult as many would have you think—but it is good to get used to the experience as there will be a few surprises for certain.

After approach to the moorings becomes easy, it is time to make weather approaches to a dock, stop, and sail away. The goal is docking, not touch and go landing. Unless a crewmember can easily step shore-side with a line in hand, it's a failure. If you are practicing single-handing, this dock person will need to be you. This will seem no trouble unless one panics.

Next; make weather approaches to the dock, and parallel park. Limit your working room between a couple of pilings, hopefully about a boat length and a half apart. You'll find that by carefully pinching and luffing you'll be able to slide in sideways. In other words, we're pointing so high that all we make is lee–way—but lee–way in the direction we want to go.

Now, sail to weather into a slip. Easy? Should be, and I'm sure it will be if you've done your practice.

Now let's start with down wind approaches. These are considerably more difficult. Obviously the trick is to keep the power down. How will you stop? There are only two ways—pure physical beef on the dock, or by surging a line around a cleat or a piling, strategically chosen. Practice your line handling and your composure. These maneuvers aren't difficult, but a failure will invariably mean a crash. Don't crash.

Not sure where you are going? Of course this means taking a sail by and checking it out. Not sure? Don't try.

MAKE SURE your spring line is strong enough, elastic enough(nylon) and irrevocably bent to your ship or you will have a disaster—again this is a skill requiring some agility but really quite easy as long as you do everything right.

Don't freak out and fall over the lifeline as you get off your boat. I've seen it happen. The worst I've seen happen, however, have been under power. A couple of times now I've seen a guy jump over the side of the boat onto the dock, the mooring line or something fouls on the throttle as he goes over the side and the boat just guns ahead…I've seen a boat go clear over the dock all the way to the forefoot this way. Very dramatic…crashes can happen—beware!

And I said SPRING LINE, right? This means led from amidships about where the center of lateral resistance is—if you clamp the brakes on too far forward the stern will flip out; too far aft the bow, although this is less dramatic. On a lot of boats, the sheet winch is pretty close.

OK, here we go.

Oh yes, for these drills—have a capable buddy on board so if you screw up or fall in the water your boat won't just sail off…And one other warning—people will see you coming in and offer a helping hand. Politely refuse. You need to learn to do this alone, and there is only one way to do that—alone. Besides, docking a boat with lines is a skill few people possess, even skill for small boats. You'll not take my advice on this and you'll see what happens. Invariably, if you let someone take your line, they'll take the bow line—and the first thing they will do is pull on it—generally perpendicular to the dock. Of course the immediate effect will be to swing to boat all out of shape, and if you're coming into a slip, the stern will swing out and you'll likely bump the boat beside you. Mark my words, they'll do this every time. Make sure your crew knows enough about line handling not to do this either. You don't need a lot of space to stop a boat even at speed with a good spring line and cleat—a foot and a half? Don't panic, shoot for high efficiency motion.

OK: We're coming into the marina slow, preferably under the main, reefed if need be—all we want is steerage. Why? A lot of guys think a headsail would be better—with the idea that you can spill it off the wind. No, that flogging headsail will still have plenty of drive off the wind. Besides, if you need to abort the maneuver the headsail will not round your boat up readily at low speeds to get yourself out of trouble. If the wind is really screaming—you'll probably going to only get one attempt under bare poles. Try to avoid this situation as maneuverability is obviously very limited.

So here we come. We want no more sail area than necessary to maintain steerage, again, right?

Approach the dock, slide up close, step ashore, and take a single turn around a dock cleat or a pile. Ease her to a halt by gradually applying tension in a single pulse—if you do it right, the boat will just scootch into her fenders and stop. If you don't she'll crash into something, of course.

With practice, you'll need about two boat lengths, not all of this needing to be dock space—as certainly your slip won't be that long. That length means a final approach and surging to a halt.

WATCH THE BOOM! If you've still got sail set, for it's really easy to whack it on a piling or a neighboring boat. If you have the boom sheeted amidships for a final dead downwind approach in moderate conditions, you'll find that that you can slow the boat quite significantly this way. The difficulty of course, is the threat of a gust from the side—certainly a possibility in a marina with a number of boat–sheds, etc., so be aware.

Be aware as well as the very significant blanketing effect that breakwaters and buildings have on wind speed, both upwind and downwind of them. Be aware that if it is blowing hard, that at low tide the apparent wind behind the breakwater will be much less than it is at high water. If you've got a difficult entrance, try to use this to your advantage.

By the way, here is the save all technique for how to get in to the impossibly tight spot, down wind, under sail. Come blazing into where you've got to go, round up, take a quick tack to where dead to weather of your chosen hole is. Drop the anchor. Dump the main sail, and pay back rode until you work yourself in. Just leave the hook on the bottom until you're ready to go; give a haul and sail off.

Now leaving a slip isn't much different, but one actually sees more crashes when people try this under sail than in docking. The reason for this is simple—as we've said, people do not anticipate the initial surge of motion of the boat before the keel bites and the rudder gains control. Again, high aspect rudder designs only make this worse as they are prone to stall at high angles of bite—one will see the boat, helmsman with the rudder hard over, just fore–reach into a piling. Be aware of this situation and again, know your boat.

One has basically just a couple of possibilities here as well. Bow in, and bow out, of course, and up wind and down wind exits.

The simplest, of course, is the bow out, down wind exit. You set your main, let slip your lines and sail out of the slip. (see the section on toggles) If you're going to have to make an immediate turn, of course set your main on the tack that facilitates that turn.

Bow out and upwind is hardly more complicated, except to say that it is generally best to let slip the lines, have your dockman give the boat a solid bob–sled running start to gain steerage, and sail off and away.

So certainly it makes a good deal of sense to keep the bow out in the slip, right? This is inconvenient, somewhat, as it isn't often reasonable to back into a slip under sail. This means at some point turning the boat around under oars or sails in mild conditions. This practice is certainly good prudent seamanship and eliminates a good deal of trouble.

Assuming we ignore this and we leave the boat in the slip bow in—then we've got difficulty. To get out of the slip is going to require oar power or line handling or something. No surprise this, and certainly traditional—this is how we go about it.

Let us say first that we are bow in, with the wind wanting to blow us out of the slip stern first. This may be an easy situation on some boats, on others difficult. If your boat will keep steerage making sternway this may be very little difficulty, even so much as you may be able to set and feather the main—or further keep it from setting through "scandalizing" it by topping up the boom and letting the leech flog. If a nudge astern is given by the dockman, a gentle bobsled start, the boat can be let out and the helm put over so the bow is pointed towards exit, hopefully, a broad reach or close—the main sheeted in gently to apply sail–power and to discourage uncontrolled fore–reaching, the boat will sail away easily.

If the stern faces out and this happens to be upwind, there is not much to be done other than to row the boat out of the slip against it, or to haul it out by lines. If the wind is too much for oars—generally about 15 knots—and lines are needed, it is probably just best to turn to boat fully around, put it back in the slip by any means accessible, and make it a much easier, bow out, upwind exit.

When sailing in confined spaces avoid these common errors:

When tacking to weather in a narrow fairway, be sure to use the full width available. Many feel uncomfortable tacking mere feet from the transoms of other boat or spiting distance from a breakwater, but this is necessary and not dangerous or reckless if one has control of one's boat. Use the full distance, maintain speed and steerage, else by pinching and tacking back and forth too short one will destroy speed and steerage, and one will loose control.

Trim the main for maximum maneuverability—this often means full sail with a slightly cupped leech on boats with cruising style underbodies.

Maintain steerage: Do not go so slow that you have poor rudder response time. Again, this varies boat to boat—again, large boats with large underbodies often retain control at very low speeds, faster boats often need more speed to retain control. Don't be so cautious that you create hazards.

Make all maneuvers clearly and with distinct intent. Realize that most boaters do not understand sail and that your actions will confuse them. Be explicit, this is basic courtesy to other boaters who need to know what you are doing. Use sound signals when appropriate. Again, recognize that even so many boaters won't understand what you are doing, and it will be dependent on YOUR skill to avoid an issue. Be prepared to settle up against a boat–shed, or pilings, or the transoms of other boats—gently and with skill, to avoid someone will less ability.

A boat with a lot of freeboard, high windage, little underbody, and a wide beam is really going to be a hassle to dock under sail.

Again, be very hesitant to accept help with your lines as it can often cause trouble.

Lastly, it will happen on occasion—although certainly rarely—that someone will gripe at you that your sailing maneuvers are reckless and dangerous. You'll immediate recognize the source of this complaint when you hear it, as it invariably comes from people of very marginal seamanlike ability and very little recognition of that—they assume that whatever must be dangerous or impossible for them must be dangerous and impossible for someone else too. The thing to do is to blow these people off. Say that you'd absolutely be in support of a policy that demanded a practical test of boat-handling ability of anyone on the water—this usually will shut them up. Don't let them worry you—these people hide in the shadows all day looking for something to complain about and you just gave them an opportunity to make their day meaningful. More often than not, rather than these, you'll meet people who are overwhelmingly appreciative of your obvious demonstration of all–too–rare ability.

Passagemaking:

In order to make the best, fastest, most efficient passage from one hypothetical harbor to another through a hypothetical group of islands, a sailor would need to know:

> The weather forecast:
> The time, and magnitude of the tide:
> The hypothetical speed advance in such conditions:

And this is modified by the chosen course, involving these local effects:

> The effects of vertical relief on the localized airflow:
> The funneling effect of predominant wind conditions in appropriately oriented channels:
> The amount of likely turbulence in the windflow, and the resultant velocity veer:
> The frictional resistance met by the wind of all weather shores:
> The frictional resistance met by the wind of all lee shores:
> Whether frictional resistance will further induce veer:
> Whether katabatic flow will be encountered:
> The likely presence of inversions and when or if they will disperse:

Whether sea breeze generation will be part of the local forecast:

And this will need to be known of every possible moment of the day, in real time, modified by the boat's present position and:

Local strategy influenced by sea state:
Local strategy influenced by channel convergence:
Local strategy influenced by channel divergence:

Head spinning from all that? It certainly should—and this of course is the reason that sailing is challenging and interesting, as opposed to motorsailing, which makes the knowledge of everything on my list inconsequential. How much difference does this knowledge make? An immense amount. Locally, we sponsor a race of 35 miles around a local island—a course complicated and that involves most all of these variables. The race rules are as thus—no engines, of course, at anytime during the weekend of the race, otherwise no handicaps. Handicaps never been needed as the course is fair, skill is far more important than the boat—and frankly we've found so few sailors who have the ability to complete the race, regardless of how "trick" or fast their boat might be. During the weekend of the race, the course can be sailed at any time the skipper of the boat chooses—but at the second the boat leaves the breakwater, the clock starts running and continues until the boat re–enters the harbor. The forecast of course is known to all, the tides indicate a good time to leave—and usually all the boats leave within a few hours of each other—often within less than an hour of each other. The results? It has been typical each year we have held the race that fully half of the fleet hasn't finished. There is generally one or two boats that make good time—I hold the course record at a little over 6 hours, a few boats will straggle in about 10 hours, and then a long last few diehards will make perhaps 16 hour times. Why? There are those who would say this is due to the pure luck of the fact of being in the right place at the right time—but since the same people have taken first, second, and third for years running, that is an unlikely explanation. No, I would say that a good deal of sailing IS the skill of being in the right place at the right time, and there is a good deal that one needs to know to be able to develop this skill.

Of course, this race never gets "called" because a good part of the fleet, though certainly not all, are engineless boats, and they're going to complete the race whether it's called or not. This changes things a bit too.

Stories abound concerning this race—generally involving someone being caught in a rip in a near calm and being stuck there for hours. The statement that is typically made is "wow, if we could have only made a hundred yards, we wouldn't have had any trouble." Of course one wouldn't—sailing, if one does it, can be mindless for a thousand miles and impossible for a hundred yards. We've discussed this: that is what makes sailing interesting, of course—those hard spots. If one has only sailed the convenient times, and puttered through those "hundred yards', one might sail 90% of the time for a lifetime but only learn 10% of what sailing is all about…

Again this book isn't the place to discuss all the aspects of meteorology that apply, except in the short form to raise the ISSUE of certain phenomenon, so the reader at least is aware of their existence and can begin to look for their effects. There are certainly other books of some detail that will deal with these issues in depth—the best ones I know of are listed on our website; **www.oarclub.org.** Still much can be said that can be applied even the next time one sails.

So then, let's discuss things a bit.

There are basically two kinds of wind—frontal and thermal. This is a gross oversimplification but will suffice for us now. Frontal wind is generated by (imagine) the motion of frontal systems and by the effect of differences in atmospheric pressure. Thermal wind is generated by the local heating of air and surfaces during the day—and has many different forms, of which simple "sea breeze" generation is typical. One can certainly have the effects of one or the other during the day, or both. Still, basically, for frontal effects one must have indication of a change in barometric pressure—and the magnitude of the change has a direct bearing on the magnitude of the effective wind. Thermal wind is dependant on change in temperature and a difference in temperature differential—and the greater this differential the greater the magnitude of the effect.

Heating of air causes air to rise. This effect is modified by temperature, humidity, and topography, but in all cases the rising of air causes a change in barometric pressure, generally relatively localized, and this is responsible for the generation of wind.

In any case, air flows horizontally from an area of high pressure to an area of lower pressure, assuming that both of these areas are of the same elevation. At the surface, wind speeds are generally the lowest, and the horizontal air flow—the wind—is effected greatly by the friction of the ground and slowed. The source altitude of windflow and the frictional attachment to the surface is very important—as it keys in effect of the earth's rotation. A surface wind has its direction is relatively unaffected by the rotation of the earth. At greater altitudes, however, the frictional effect of the surface is negligible. At these levels the airflow retains the rotational velocity of the of the surface of the earth at its point of origin and flows from that point with a COMBINED speed dependant on BOTH the pressure gradient AND the earth's location. Airflow at progressively higher altitudes is progressively skewed from its direct course from the high pressure to low pressure point by the Coriolis effect of the rotation of the earth. In the Northern Hemisphere this means that flow at high altitudes is increasingly deviated in a clockwise fashion—veered—as compared to the surface flow. The converse would be the case in the Southern Hemisphere. If for some reason pockets of this upper level airflow reaches the surface, the wind at the surface will be veered relative to the original direction of flow. This airflow will reach the surface for a number of reasons, pure turbulence, thermal effects, etc., but the effect remains the same and of immediate interest to the sailor: surface airflow will veer increasingly over time in a strong airflow that is relatively stable—if the airflow is UNSTABLE, the surface airflow will be mixed with occasional gusts of upper level airflow which will appear veered relative to the airflow at the surface. These observations give us important clues.

With frontal systems, strong winds are associated with the *edges of high pressure systems*, and located with the *center of low pressure systems*. As these systems move across the surface, surface airflow encountering frictional resistance or topography is deflected, this deflection creates eddies and turbulence that brings upper level air to the surface. Calms on the other hand can be associated with very little barometric gradient, but usually are surface effects caused by inversions—these caused by vertical stability, vertical stability caused by the lack of significant thermal action. If the airflow over the inversion is very stable with little turbulence, calms are likely to occur and persist.

While observation of the actual behavior of the wind at present gives some indication of what is to come—observations at distance can be made by observing the formation of behavior of clouds. Clouds can tell us much about the weather—it can tell us if the weather forecast we may have received is holding true, as well can it tell us much about effects that might be occurring on more of a local scale. Clouds are certainly useful to the sailor in many ways: let's discuss them a bit.

Cloud formation, like wind, is influenced by one of two factors—thermal action or the presence of a front. Cloud formation on a local scale is generally caused by thermal action. As sunlight heats a surface, the air on that surface gets heated as well because of conduction. Thus that air expands and begins to rise. As the air rises, it generally expands as it encounters less pressure with altitude. As gasses expand, the law of conservation of energy dictates that they must cool, and cool they do—at a more or less uniform rate. This rate of cooling is known as the Adiabatic Lapse Rate—generally meaning a cooling of about 1 degree centigrade for every 100 meters of elevation gain.

As our column of rising air rises, it does so to seek a layer of equal density as relative to the surrounding air. How far this column of air is able to rise is dependant on how high that area of equal density might be in the surrounding air. If the gradient(also called lapse rate) of the surrounding air is less than the Adiabatic Lapse Rate, meaning that the air temperature decreases *less with altitude*, the heated air will rise only a short distance before it reaches air of like density and will rise no further. If an atmospheric inversion is present—meaning an ambient area of *negative lapse rate, an increase in temperature with altitude*—the rise of the column of air will cease at that elevation. If the lapse rate of the surrounding air is greater than the Adiabatic Lapse Rate, the column of heated air will rise and continue to rise as long as this remains the case. At some point the cooling of the air will force condensation to occur, this condensation will cause cloud cover to be formed—and this cloud cover indicative of this effect.

Otherwise cloud cover tells of the presence, motion, and proximity of a front. Even more, they tell what sort of front is approaching—whether a warm front or a cold front.

So then, what do we read in the skies?

Types of clouds:

Cirrus:

The whispy, feathery streaks of cloud that appear at high altitudes are called cirrus clouds. Comprised mostly of ice, they are not substantive enough to block much sunlight and are more or less transparent. They are associated with the approach of a warm front, and the action of the warm front as it climbs over and pushes back colder air at the surface.

"Mare's tail's" are a form of cirrus cloud.

The appearance of cirrus clouds themselves are an indication of the depth of the depression that brings them. The more regular and pervasive they are, the more likely bad weather is imminent. The more drawn and windblown cirrus clouds appear, the more upper–atmospheric wind is present.

Cirrostratus:

Cirrostratus is associated with a warm front or low–pressure systems more immediate presence—as it comes closer the cirrus becomes more pronounced and covers the entire sky in a thin screen. At this point it is known as cirrostratus. Cirrostratus is associated as well with sun dogs, halos around the sun and moon—and other effects of atmospheric refraction. Cirrostratus indicates that the front is quite close and getting closer.

Cirrocumulus:

As the cirrus gets denser with the further approach of the warm front, small, individually distinct clouds begin to appear. This cirrocumulus cloud is now thick enough in places to block some sunlight and will cause a rippled appearance in the sky. This is the famous "mackerel sky" that sailors of old spoke of. It means, yet again, that the warm front is at one's doorstep.

Altostratus:

The next cloud that typically might appear as the warm front comes in is the altostatus. A gray, uniform sheet at a lower altitude—altostratus is dense enough to diffuse sunlight more or less completely. It indicates yet again the immediate presence of the warm front and rain that it brings with it.

Stratus:

Stratus appears much the same as altostratus but is present at yet a lower altitude and is denser yet and usually darker. Sometimes stratus rolls in as a uniform sheet in the sky, sometimes as large patches of cloud with breaks of sun between them. If associated with wind, which it often may be, it is often broken up and is referred to by sailors as "scud"—scud often indicates the high likely–hood of a low pressure storm.

Nimbostratus:

Nimbostratus means stratus that is associated with rain. It is the thick, dark, featureless cloud cover that brings rain or snow. It is typically associated, again, with rain, a rapid fall in barometric pressure, and indicates that the front is no longer approaching but has arrived. The thing for a sailor to watch for at this point is a directional veer in the wind, as it indicates the passage of this front and the hopeful improvement of weather behind. If the wind backs, it generally means that another low pressure system may be riding the coattails of this one and that one should not expect an immediate improvement.

The immediate improvement of weather associated with a veering wind and clearing skies occurs when the area of a low pressure system called the "warm sector" is present. The "warm sector" is the area of the low pressure system that lies behind the warm front as it advances and the cold front that follows it. It generally brings much clearer skies, sunshine, and the end of precipitation.

Altocumulus:

Altocumulus clouds are round, globular clouds at moderate altitude—"sheepswool" fluffy clouds with only moderate shading and density. They are generally associated with clear sky and fair weather. They are associated with the presence of the warm sector we just spoke of, but are also associated with thermal lifting of air and its resultant condensation. At any rate, they indicate the presence of instability in the mid–atmosphere, and with the resultant wind conditions, i.e., gusty.

Stratocumulus:

If the atmosphere has more stability than in the last case, altocumulus often forms together into large, long, parallel bands of cloud that cover all or most of the sky. It becomes lower, heavier, and denser than typical altocumulus. It may indicate the presence of large atmospheric inversions. If it is dark enough, it indicates rain. At any rate, it generally indicates little surface wind until it passes.

Cumulonimbus:

As the warm front is driven away by the invasion of the following cold front, large–scale vertical lifting is stimulated and this carries a good deal of cloud into the upper atmosphere. Cumulonimbus are the large, towering clouds we associate with thunderstorms, squalls, and the like. Their presence means the immediate presence of the cold front, perhaps within hours. One should expect the local squalls to pass, but the ambient wind to strengthen and veer—this means the cold front has arrived.

Cumulus:

As the cold front passes and the high–pressure system behind it enters the area, it often carries with it the large, heap clouds known at cumulus. Mid to low altitude clouds, they indicate atmospheric convection and a good deal of atmospheric instability. They appear and disappear as the moisture in them is condensed, absorbed, and dissipated in the eddies of convected wind aloft. This atmospheric instability is likely to meet the surface in the form of strong, gusty wind

So then, what can we learn from this?

A sailor can expect a good deal of wind whenever the atmospheric pressure gradient is large. The motion in the barometer tells us this tale, and local effects do too. Sudden changes in wind velocity are good clues. Sudden changes in wind velocity *and* temperature especially so. Sudden changes in wind velocity and temperature often cause sudden changes in cloud structure and cover and are good indications as well.

Indications of atmospheric instability also indicate wind. Remember that strong winds more often come *down* than *in*. Cumulus cloud, again, is a good indication of instability.

Atmospheric instability is enhanced by surface heating. Surface heating, of course, generates vertical airflow, and this generates turbulence, allowing stronger, mid–altitude winds to find the surface.

On the other hand, if there is very little pressure gradient, once cannot expect much wind (or sailing). If little variation in temperature occurs during the day, little sea–breeze generation is likely to occur either.

If one is experiencing socked in rain in the middle of a depression, it is unlikely that any significant wind will appear either.

If the atmospheric stability is very strong—or an inversion is present—little wind can be expected to find the surface.

Inversions are often typical of areas that have relatively warm air and cold water—as the water cools the surface air—causing a negative lapse rate—and thus the "inversion." This cold, relatively dense air is stable and lies on the surface of the water like a pool, the upper level air does not have the turbulence or density to sink through it and reach the surface—so calms persist. Conduction inversions such as the one described are often obvious when viewing smokestacks, as the smoke rises it does so vertically until it reaches a certain altitude where it suddenly sheers off.

These conditions are likely to persist if cloud cover is total, for it often takes surface heating to create the instability to drive inversions out.

Of course one can only sail when there is wind...

All of these large scale phenomena are altered by local effects, but fortunately in relatively predictable ways. Wind encountering topography will either be slowed or accelerated—it will be slowed most by obstacles with large amounts of friction—like a wooded hillside, and will be allowed to accelerate as it leaves land and travels out across water. A wind leaving land and traveling over water is modified depending on its stability characteristics. If the wind is unstable, the experienced surface wind will be most pronounced at the windward shore because this is where the greatest eddying action occurs. If the wind is relatively stable, the wind will leave the shoreline at approximately the height of the shoreline, so that the area immediately near the weather shore will be a blanketed calm.

As the wind approaches a shore to leeward, on the other hand, it tends to encounter the shore with a flow oriented to run over the obstacles immediate the shoreline. Depending on how stable the airflow is, a blanketed area will occur some distance from this shore as well.

Not only does airflow velocity change as it approaches or leaves a shoreline, but it also often changes direction. If the airflow leaves a shoreline at an angle oblique to the wind front the direction will change to more perpendicular to the shoreline. This effect, again, is more pronounced in stable flow than in unstable flow. If the airflow encounters a lee shore at an oblique angle, the windflow generally alters to travel parallel to it. Again, this effect is more pronounced in air that is stable than that which is turbulent.

Thus, in very stable airflow wind, such as that generated by sea breeze, it tends to channel itself and flow along shorelines, and in turbulent air it tends more likely to follow the directional tendency of the front that drives it.

So then, of immediate use to the sailor are these observations. First of all, knowing a basic forecast and what is to be expected, indicators tell stories of what is afoot. Winds that are backing, or shifting counterclockwise(in the Northern Hemisphere)—are threatening to die. Winds with gusts that are veering are likely to strengthen, or at any rate not die. There is also the very practical importance of the fact that when sailing to weather on a starboard tack, gusts will be lifts—and will aid the speed of the boat, while on the port tack gusts will be headers. Therefore, it is good practice for a Northern Hemisphere sailor to favor the starboard tack as his long board if he can, for this tack will give the greatest speed of advance.

If one is becalmed, little is going to change without a serious change in temperature, either of the air or the water. Most importantly, there needs to be a difference generated in the temperature above the water as opposed to the temperature above the land. One can certainly watch for this to occur. Cloud cover makes this unlikely, of course, and one can only hope for wind generated for the cooling of night.

Tall objects create blanketing effects, both to leeward and to weather as the air must lift from the surface to flow over them. In stable air, the blanket to leeward of an obstruction can be as far as thirty times the height of the obstruction. The blanket to weather of an obstruction in stable air can be as far as ten times the height of the obstruction. In unstable air, the blanket to leeward of an obstruction is shortened to perhaps five times its height, and a windward blanket may not appear at all.

When sailing to weather in a channel where the wind is more or less following parallel to the shoreline, it is best to try to orient one's tacks to take advantage of the lifts generated at the ends of points along the shore. If one does not, the alternative is to be perpetually headed. If the channel is converging, this is pronounced, so sail close in, shore to shore. If the channel is diverging, so will the wind flow, so try to tack short in the middle of the channel to again avoid being headed.

Sea breeze generation is not going to happen without sun, and before it does, usually some sort of cloud cover will appear inland as its precursor. This cloud cover, especially over hilltops, indicates vertical movement of air due to heating and horizontal airflow is soon to follow.

If the frontal wind is parallel to the shoreline, sea breeze generation will generally be diminished, as the temperature differential is simply blown out of the area.

Hillsides facing the sun heat sooner than flat ground and generate sea breeze most quickly.

If in doubt, and facing a calm, the old adage is "seek the shore." This is good advice from a number of different counts. First, if there is current to be encountered, it is very likely to be less pronounced in shallow water. Secondly, any breeze to be had, especially a sea breeze, is likely to last just off shore the longest. Lastly, if all else fails, and one is becalmed, any shoreline becomes an anchorage, so simply drop the hook and have dinner…just be prepared to leave when the wind comes back up.

If we look at high altitude clouds, i.e., stratus—we can see that they stream in more or less the direction of the upper level flow. Mid–level clouds, however, form more in waves—rows or lines perpendicular to the weather system flow. Much can be learned from this. If one observes the direction of the surface flow, one can expect that the surface flow will be backed (relative to the mid–level flow, as indicated by the orientation of the cloud bands) to some degree because its speed is retarded by surface friction. How much depends on a number of factors—but between 15 and 30 degrees may be typical. If this expected backing is not present—it indicates that the atmospheric effect observed are more of a local nature—likely caused by thermal convection, and the passage of a depression or a front is not a important determinant in the present conditions.

When one sees upper level clouds crossing the sky in a different direction than the lower level clouds—the conditions that dictate the behavior of the upper level clouds will soon prevail over all.

Sea birds seem to have an uncanny sense of what the weather will bring—if they don't see fit to leave their roosts, neither should you…

Lastly, remember that change in tide generally involves a change in water temperature, and this may be just enough to encourage a change in the weather that is about to happen to make itself known. Calms often appear and disappear within a half–hour of the change of the tide, and since this can be predicted locally often with great precision, is an excellent indicator of good times to leave, or especially, be inside, a harbor. Be aware, however, that as one feels the first stirring of the breeze to not be carried away with this rapture—many times this has occurred to me in the dark hours of the morning and I harden up the sheets to take advantage of this new wind only to nearly have a collision with a floating log in the very change in tide that brought the wind…

Heavy Weather Techniques:

When one reads older sailing books one often hears of being "caught out" in a blow, and the subject is given a good deal of treatment. For good reason, as well, for fifty years ago even those yachts equipped with inboard engines has propulsion that was capable of little more than dealing with calms, and it was assumed that the "blow" would have to be dealt with under sail—requiring a good deal of seamanship. Today, this is seldom the case among cruising boats. Most have very substantial engine power and large propellers capable of providing control and steerage up to a full gale—some even more that this—and has made the seamanship involved in handling sail in difficult circumstances much less important. As such, the expectations of people and the strategies they apply to their boats has changed.

What a "blow" might be has a good deal to do with a boat and its crew. A solid, well–designed sailboat—even a small one—with a strong crew can make way to weather in force 7 relatively reliably, and as such—while these conditions may cause for a good deal of inconvenience, cause relatively little hazard. Truth be known, however, a true force 7 wind is a strong wind—and actually uncommon especially in the season that people desire to do their sailing. It is resultant of significant enough effects that it seldom will occur without prior forecast or warning. It would be difficult for a sailor, familiar with the signs of weather, to miss a gale's approach.

Let me state flatly that seamanship is much better demonstrated by avoiding the gale than by weathering it—although the account of the former is much less interesting than the narrative of the latter. Yet again it is best to avoid the issue altogether. If one is to do some cruising, it is bound to happen that one will find oneself in a situation where one will have to deal with more wind than one would like, and it is wise to have the skills to do so.

There are in essence three places one can face heavy weather—in a harbor, tided to a study dock, in an anchorage of some security, or underway. Each carries its own hazards. Let us discuss these.

The primary hazard encountered by a sailor who is stormbound in a good safe harbor is overindulgence and the resultant headache. As such, the harbor is much to be preferred.

An anchorage is different. Upon entering an anchorage in a sailboat, one must make a careful decision about what one's strategy will be if conditions take a turn for the worst. This question is whether the anchorage is secure in a blow or not. Some are, and some are not. The determining factors are the quality of the holding, the amount of wave action the anchorage will experience, and the number of other boats present. At any rate, it is not prudent for a sailboat to seek the obvious snug, in–close spot in the anchorage—it is wise to keep some sea room—unless one is preparing for a full–blown storm. One will not have a boat drag down on them if they anchor to weather—leaving the anchorage is kept a simple prospect as well. This may not be convenient, but it is prudent—and prudence is the key. Obviously in settled weather this is little of a concern, but boats will drag in as little as 20 knots of air and this could be a hassle. Pay attention, and always think ahead.

I have been forced to leave anchorages a number of times—an anchorage that would have been secure became irresponsibly crowded—the wind came up, and chaos ensued. It is an exciting event, to be sure, to hoist a main, sound a horn, and sail out of tight anchorage in the middle of the night under the light of a handheld spot–light—but I would often rather be underway to other places than deal with hours of being forced to watch other boats—all surging around on inadequate ground tackle, all on inadequate scope. As a sailboat, I have no recourse but to sail. To be entangled in another boat's rode and dragged ashore would more or less leave me helpless. Still, little harm would likely occur unless the conditions were really serious, but it is often simpler and easier to take advantage of the wind and be underway to one's next port. If conditions were likely to be that serious—I hope I would have been someplace else—and frankly, it is unlikely that the anchorage I was in would have been crowded. Still, the point remains, there are good anchorages for a storm and many that are not. Be sure one chooses wisely.

If anchoring against disaster, and one has resolved to stay at all costs, setting two bow anchors is greatly more secure than one. Drag them both in against the load of a kedge and leave the kedge on deck, coiled and ready. Obviously the ambient load on each is halved, but more importantly the boat will swing less and less load will come in surges. It is unlikely to drag both anchors. As they swing less ground chafe will be lessened. Of course, it is important to have a good idea of what direction the wind will be coming from during the storm, but at any rate having two anchors set is a good idea for an boat that must rely on them. Watch for chafe! It is prudent to use a couple of rope snubbers to carry the load save the wear and tear on the anchor rode itself.

Being underway in a blow may become plenty wet, uncomfortable, and fatiguing—but as long as one can make way to weather there is little hazard. Baring this, as long as one has sea–room, there is little hazard. A sailor's strategy should take these two factors into account immediately. That is, to make as much way to weather as one can—in anticipation that one might not be able to later. As well, to choose a course that allows one room to run if one must.

Of course, this all describes being caught out in a "blow"—not being caught out in apocalypse. If that happens, you're simply out of luck and must hope for the best.

So then, being caught out in difficult conditions—it is good to consider:

> How long the conditions will last:
> How bad the conditions will get:
> If there are harbors I can make in these conditions:
> If there are not harbors, are there areas I can sail into to avoid some of the worst of it?
> If there are any areas I must avoid because wind and tide may make them especially bad?

And hopefully there will be good answers to all of these.

Again there, is much said about being caught out in a "blow." There are techniques applicable to each type of boat, and the area one sails in. The point I want to emphasize, however, is this: the key is being prepared. If gear is unstowed, chaos will ensue. If one is unfamiliar with one's storm canvas—trouble will arise. If one hasn't adequate charts—one's options of places to hide will be greatly diminished—and running into an unknown bay would be foolhardy.

Although this book is written from the perspective of coastal or inland sailing—some deep sea techniques are still of use. Namely, that would be streaming warps. It will often become important to keep a boat's speed down, for as much to remain safe in a seaway and avoid broaching, as simply reducing a boats speed to avoid running off all of one's sea room. It is much simpler to keep a boat under control at low speeds than high—it is much easier to navigate at low speeds than high as well. There are conditions, however, that recommend making good time. Although running for harbor has probably sunk more boats than it has saved—I have done so, after making careful decisions, and am still here to tell about it. Again, it is very tempting when facing the prospect of hours of slogging around in the wind and spray to want to get it all over with—but one must face this reality with discipline and honesty. Always choose the safe course. The times I ran for harbor I did so because it was the *safe* option...

Never ever, ever, *ever* forget about the presence of any lee shore. In large inland waters, of course, this is everywhere. It is the lee shore that was the terror of the past and it is certainly still a threat, although some modern boats have the capacity to make way to weather in conditions that older boats would have been forced to run.

Make sure you have good solid weather canvas, and that you have a rig and a *hull* that could take twenty hours of hard driving to weather. I don't believe a lot of boats are up to this kind of task. Take the boat out sailing sometime and deliberately over–canvas it—really lean on it hard. With someone else at the helm, go below and sniff around every bulkhead and chain–plate—try to find anything that creaks at all. If you find something, make a note, and beef it up. You need confidence in the boat. Nothing should budge. Fiberglass is cheap.

Remember as well that everything that is above the waterline that isn't sail area will be trying to drive you onto that lee shore, and you'll have to drive the boat just that much harder for every piece of windage your boat has. Keen on mast steps, multi–spreader rigs, radar, spray dodgers, etc.?

Lastly—don't overestimate your own ability and especially *stamina*. This experience is going to be tough…

Sailing in Light Air:

Often far more troublesome than storms is the necessity of the sailor to deal with calms. A calm can be as potentially as dangerous as a storm in areas with a good deal of ship traffic—barring this calms are certainly a good deal more pervasive and unpredictable. Still, a true Force 0 calm is uncommon, but a practical calm of Force 1 is not. A sailboat must be equipped to make way in these conditions. Most sailboats are not.

First and foremost one requires a great deal of sail area. There is no way to escape this. Large genoa jibs, spinnakers, etc., are the key. Large sails are always to some degree inconvenient, but when compared with long hours of rowing a heavy boat, most sailors will welcome their inconvenience.

There are many ways to equip a boat to carry more sail. Some sailor rig jib–boom arrangements or temporary bowsprits that carry special light air sails, or flying jibs. This increases the potential sail area greatly. Asymmetrical cruising spinnakers are excellent, as it is often especially difficult to maintain steerage off the wind. As large as possible and in as light as cloth as possible is the right choice for these conditions.

Tall masts are an aid, but they detract from performance in heavy air, and for many boats that cruise year round are probably not a good idea, especially when other options such as a jib–boom exist.

It may be often found that in light air, certain courses will not be able to be sailed, especially off the wind. If there is a good deal of chop or powerboat wakes, one might not be able to keep one's sails set on the wind. Try to find a course that one can sail—and sail it to maintain steerage. Head for a plausible anchorage, as everything becomes an anchorage in Force 0. Pay especial attention to traffic, and to current—as these become serious problems without steerage.

The effects of current become pronounced—so use current to aid one's apparent wind. If sailing with a tide against a wind, one might find that one can maintain reasonable steerage, but one might not be able to in the opposite direction. Sailing downwind with a tide makes it unlikely to maintain steerage—perhaps this isn't a problem and one can just drift—but again be highly aware of issues that can arise.

Boats with slick underbodies will fare much better in light air, as will any boat if it is lightly loaded. Do a nice job on the bottom paint and maintain it. All of the dingy sailor's tricks, such as heeling the boat to leeward to aid in sail set are just as functional on a large boat as a small one—so give it a try.

Boats with a good deal of form stability and a wide beam will have trouble keeping sails set if there is little wind and a chop. Narrow, ballast keel boats will fare better.

Often the key to sailing to weather is to get way on and keep it on—as long as one can keep speed on one will keep steerage. A single powerboat wake, however, can often stop one dead. It is entirely practical to break out an oar and get a knot back on again, where one may find that sailing is once again possible.

Patience and deliberate sailing is the key.

I think for most boats light air canvas of at least twice the square footage of the working sails is critical. More for heavy boats, less for light boats—not all of this needs to be able to be carried to weather but it does off the wind. That would mean perhaps 800 to 900 square feet on a typical 30 foot boat is an excellent start.

Necessary Gear for Voyaging:

Sails:

As difficult as it is to find well proportioned boat—it is almost as difficult to find well proportioned sails. When one enters a sail loft and inquires of sails, the first question that comes from the sailmaker is this—is one racing or cruising? A nonsensical question when one considers it—are the demands of a sail for racing and cruising different? Does a cruiser want slow sails for some purpose? Practically speaking—there IS a difference between racing and cruising sails though there need not be—and wasn't thirty years ago. Today racing is only done in controlled circumstances and the range of conditions that a race boat encounters is quite narrow. Cruising today is generally done by those less than vital and less than experienced and sails are given more abuse and neglect than they might have thirty years ago when many sailors had habits acquired from the era of cotton. Thus cruising sails are often built too heavy and stiff with anticipation of this abuse. What one needs on an sailboat are highly versatile sails cut much like racing sails, but out of dacron rather than laminates so as to keep that versatility, built a bit heavier than a typical racing sail, but not built like a typical cruising sail. The shape should be optimal, as it is not the case in cruising sails typically—optimized sails require more attention at the helm and most cruisers are not willing to give that attention. There are lofts that will cut fast sails of dacron and not suggest full battens—that know what a fine entry and 50 percent draft chord means—but not many—and fewer yet that will listen when one asks for it. One can find these lofts, however if one looks.

I really think the best answer for the self–sufficient sailor is to build one's sails, either from kits or from scratch—although precut kits are generally very cost effective and simple. It will be necessary if one intends to do any sort of extended cruising to learn to do sail repair—it is easiest to learn to do this by making sails right off the bat. There is surprisingly little to making sails anymore, as the issue of good sail shape has been greatly simplified by the improvements in cloth. Modern cloth is so stable as opposed to cloth of even a few years ago that the magic and the judgements involved in making sails decades ago has been made largely inapplicable—handiwork is far more of a detail and no–one cares as much about the sail as the sailor whose life will depend on it.

A reasonably solid home machine is certainly capable of handling most sail–making tasks. Most home machines can handle cloth of up to about 9 ozs. in weight—or a heavy working jib for a thirty foot boat. With some modification of a heavier balance wheel, etc., some can take more, but actually a 9 oz sail is a pretty heavy one and it is unlikely that one will see heavier than that except for special circumstances. The sewing itself can be greatly aided by soaking the thread cone in dry silicone lubricant, as this lubricates the thread and the machine, and makes for much more even tension.

How to work the cloth through the machine? In sections, with the sail rolled up like a scroll. I use two sections of four inch SD PVC pipe with a slot ripped along the length as clamps to hold it together. The PVC clamps slide over the sail, and easily feed through the machine. It makes the delicate task of broad seaming easy.

Now comes the question of what kind of wardrobe do you want? Of course we often get some sort of sails when we purchase a boat, but at some point these will need replacing and it is useful to think of what we'd like. The mistake I see most people make is to invest in a good deal of ultra–heavy duty heavy weather sails. Now there is nothing wrong with storm sails, and if one has the need for them, there is no argument against them. Yet a storm trysail on a boat that hasn't yet been outside of its home bay is a little silly, and unneeded expense. More important that these, especially for the beginner who is learning on a straight sailing boat are good *light air sails.* A powerful genoa, a cruising spinnaker or gennaker, these are to be found much more often useful than the spitfire jib. Start there. For me, I carry two spinnakers, an enormous flying jib, a 175 genoa, a working headsail of a 110 that has a set of reef points in it to reef to a 90, a storm jib, a main with two sets of reef points in it. No need that I can see for a third, as at this point we're well into trysail territory and a hell of a lot of wind. No sense in destroying the upper half of the main. This works for me, although at times I drool for even yet a larger light air genoa—and will likely build it this spring. Remember, you'll need to make way in Force 1 from here on out or you'll get to row.

As to the hazards associated with spinnakers—yes, every concern is valid. They are big, powerful sails, and can really screw up if mishandled. Most of the spinnaker handling advice comes from the racing set which generally has more and more energetic hands on board than a cruising boat might. Cruisers call for different handling techniques.

The easiest way to use a spinnaker, in my opinion, is much like a rocket engine. Point the boat in the direction you want to go and light it off. I set up the pole and both sheets before I make the hoist: I never tack it, I douse it and set it again on the opposite tack. This greatly tames things. If you swing it in behind the mainsail it will deflate and is easier yet.

Another thing I've done is install a couple of chocks on the foredeck that I can lay the pole to act as a bowsprit—much like one sees on the high dollar race sleds. I rigged a downhaul on it to keep it from lifting. I often set the chute out on this—about six feet in front of the boat—basically like one does an asymmetrical spinnaker. This is my save–all light air technique, they used to call this sort of thing a jib–boom on old traditional boats. I can set another light flying jib on it over the genoa in light air as well. Gosh, it works good, but it means for a helacious lot of sail area and it could potentially get really out of hand. Yet the things one will do to not have to row…

Now, before you get excited, I wouldn't even dream of this kind of handling if my boat were much bigger. I can manhandle this sail. On a bigger boat I couldn't, certainly not alone.

You haven't sailed yet unless you've carried your spinnaker over your big lapper in good conditions. Good God! That's moving!

While we're on it, my favorite spinnaker trick in light air is to simply take one sheet to the cleat on the foredeck and the other to the cleat on the quarter—forget poles and all, and just blow the thing out there like a kite. This is really nice when there's a bunch of powerboats madly tearing around, and a pretty good roll running. You can a lot of times get that thing to set way out in front of the boat so it doesn't chafe on anything. Surprising how well this works—but you'll start to think about the jib–boom pole system I just described. You wouldn't think it would set but it does, as long as you're running broad on the wind. Dead down it doesn't—but I almost never run dead down wind anyway. Take the main down too, or its flopping around will chafe your nerves.

Oars

Oars and sailboats are a natural combination—sailing vessels with oars go back almost as far as recorded history. No surprise that we should find them useful; the surprise is that they aren't required gear on *every* boat—engine or no. What other piece of gear is ready to be pressed into service as: 1) propulsion 2)spare spar 3) shoring member 4) extra or emergency rudder 5) fending pole 6)depth finder 7)exercise equipment? Think your boat is too large to be moved by sweeps? You've got delusions of grandeur—the US Brig Niagara carries sweeps, 40 footers, and we'll bet your yacht comes in a tad less than 300 ton…

What is the rudder but a specialized oar? You've already got one—get at least a spare…

Practically speaking, a 8000 pound boat can be rowed by one healthy person at about a knot and a half. If you've got crew to spare, you might row at two knots for brief periods of twenty minutes or so—which can often be enough to sneak you into a bay that you would have drifted by otherwise. One handed rowing or sculling can move a boat along at a knot for hours on end—not saying it's fun, but it will keep you in the middle of a channel as you ride a tide or move you out of a shipping lane if you've been stranded there. A good pull with a pair of sweeps will get your boat out of a harbor with ease in wind up to about 15 knots—more than that and you'd have trouble pulling dead into it—but that's where the seamanship comes in—leave before the wind comes up like sailors did (do). You'll also find that with a combination of rowing and sailing you can work through some amazingly tight courses.

You've got a couple of choices about oars—you can go with sweeps or plan to scull. It depends on the boat which is more effective. Sweeps offer the advantages of being shorter, more effective at turning the boat, more powerful with higher speed potential—if you break one you've still got another—and you can use them to back up and as brakes to slow yourself down. Sculling, some say, is less work. I personally advocate sweeps but it's a preference issue.

You've got choices as to make. I've got ash sweeps. They make great aluminum and carbon fiber oars for drift boats that are very nice and not crazy expensive. You can get them as one piece jobs or break down varieties. I've used them, and I think they are very fine. Would make for good choices if you'll need to stow them below deck.

You might have heard formulas for sizing oars to your boat. They're nonsense, so don't visit the wooden boat forum then go out and order a pair. Generally, your sweeps will end up being in the neighborhood of 1.5 times your beam, but this will depend on the height of your freeboard, how tall you are, how you plan to face as you row, and where you're going to stow them. Get a chunk of PVC pipe as a fake oar and see what's comfy—chop it off to that length and see where you can stow it—then order that size. Otherwise you're looking for trouble. A sculling oar is going to be a good bit longer than a sweep—basically as long as you can deal with—not a trivial issue.

A number of engineless boat people have made oar locks that fit into the top of their winches so consider that possibility if your winches have deep sockets. The winches are often placed about right.

I think standing up facing forward is a good way to row. A lot of work boats were and are rowed in that manner but with oars long enough to cross in front of you—giving a good deal more leverage.

When rowing a heavy boat, remember that nothing is going to happen quickly. You can pull to beat hell and the boat is still going to move relatively slowly. Think thrust, not speed. You'll find that short, alternating strokes will often get way on and off quicker than others, as they provide continuous thrust, not bursts, so try that. Remember that in a sailboat, you're always sailing whether you've got oars out or no—you'll find that sailing sideways into a slip with one oar pumping to keep the boat from rounding up or falling off is really no trouble. Don't be casual about dropping an oar over the side to slow yourself at speed as it will very nearly rip you right out of the cockpit—you'll gain a new appreciation for sail power and the thrust it generates.

Lastly—I advocate ALWAYS having the oars out and ready on entering and exiting marinas—but not for the reason you might think. I have learned that when people see you enter a marina under sail—they assume you've got the engine running and are "just practicing" or some such—and will power right over the top of you in most inconsiderate ways—especially this one: pass you because you're slow, then stop in front of you to ready mooring lines and fenders. This happens all the time. BUT, when you've got those sweeps out and dipping—whether you're using them or not, they get noticed and they're a very effective daymark saying "I've got no engine." People will then respect that (or be worried) and actually display some seamanship and courtesy.

Self–steering gear

Steering a boat for hours and hours, shorthanded or alone becomes incredibly tedious—and it doesn't take long for a sailor to begin to think of ways to eliminate the task. Popularly, two solutions present themselves, autopilots and windvanes. Both are expensive and complex—both unattractive to my eye at least—the autopilot noisy, complicated, and has excessive power demands for my boat; the windvane, costly, heavy, and more moving parts than I want to need to maintain. My solution? To teach my self the ancient art of natural self steering.

For me, I tried fiddling with natural course stability—this didn't work. I tried a dedicated steering sail—this worked but was clumsy. I even built a wind–vane—a horizontal axis vane, this worked as well but again was irritating to look at and didn't steer the kind of course I wanted it too. Finally, I spent a good deal of time studying sheet to tiller set ups—learned that skill, and this is what I have used solely ever since.

One needs some sort of self–steering gear—vanes are indeed tempting, but you own it to yourself before you got out and buy one that you give sheet to tiller steering a good hard try.

I'll walk through this real slow—the concept is simple but counter-intuitive, and frankly disproves a good deal of what we've been told about boats and course stability. Listen carefully: sheet to tiller steering works—it works as well or better than a vane, there is no kinda working about it. It is utterly reliable if applied properly. It cannot fail. Yet, if applied incorrectly, it doesn't work at all. Learning sheet to tiller steering was one of the most interesting and rewarding projects that I've ever encountered—certainly it was the project that has taught me more about sailing than anything else I've ever done. To develop a good, workable, sheet to tiller system DEMANDS that one actually understands what one's boat does and why—a truism perhaps, but I don't know of any other aspect of sailing that makes that demand so insistently. One can sail and make good passages with proficiency without understanding—I'm afraid I discovered I'd done that. Even if one has no need for sheet to tiller steering I recommend any sailor dabble with it simply to learn. It is an absolutely fascinating study.

There are a couple of misconceptions about what sheet to tiller steering is. Sheet to tiller steering is NOT simply tying the helm off to something while sailing to weather. As we will see—one hardly even needs to do that. It is also NOT something that "pretty much" holds a course. Unless the system holds a course as well or BETTER than a helmsman, it isn't a system. Third—a sheet to tiller system isn't a "system"—it is a skill—one that can be transported to most any boat and cobbled together out of most any parts. It is worthwhile to have a nice bag of gear—the quality of one's pieces make a very substantial improvement to the "tightness" of the course steered—but I recommend practicing with junky blocks so one learns WHY good blocks and low stretch line work better here.

Lastly, sheet to tiller system isn't and doesn't have much to do with natural course stability—that is, the much exaggerated ability of some boats to hold a course with no feedback to the helm. We will see why.

Let's once again talk about sailing. As far as sheet to tiller steering is concerned there are really only two courses—upwind and downwind. Let's keep upwind in our minds first because it is the simplest and requires the least help from the a self steering system. After we talk about upwind systems, run back through the mantras and think about downwind.

A) On any point of sail—upwind or downwind—as the boat turns to weather APPARENT WIND INCREASES. Let this be your first mantra. Many people, even those who have sailed a lifetime, do not understand this basic principle. Many confuse this statement with luffing—I am not talking about luffing nor to I have any interest in designing a system to luff. What I am talking about is that when due to change in course or shift in wind direction, as the boat turns to weather, apparent wind increases. This is due to the basic fact that boat speed remains relatively constant due to momentum. Obviously, again, if the sails stall, the boat slows down and apparent wind diminishes—but before the stall occurs—again APPARENT WIND INCREASES.

The converse is also true. As the boat turns off the wind APPARENT WIND DECREASES. No problems yet, right?

B) As heel increases—a boat—ANY BOAT—has a tendency to turn to weather. Heel is the also the PRIMARY force that turns a boat to weather. We've all been sold a bunch of bad information this business and been told a lot about asymmetry of hull bottoms and the like. Sure, there is a difference between boats. Some boats heel a lot, some not too much. Some do have lumpy bottoms. Still, all of that isn't nearly as important as the fact that as a boat heels—the center of effort—the hypothetical center of all forces acting on the boat gets swung way over the side (of the center of resistance, I suppose) and this makes the boat want to turn. It is no different than having a car with one driving axle that sticks way out to one side—that car would want to turn like crazy.

OK: This is why many boats will pretty much sail to weather with the helm lashed in steady conditions—they all have pretty much natural stability. As a boat falls off the wind and the sheets aren't trimmed, much drive turns to drag and the boat heels more, this heeling makes the boat turned back to weather. If there is a little bit of rudder angle applied making the boat always want to turn off the wind just a little bit—then somewhere an equilibrium is reached and a course is more or less held. No big deal, and most any boat will do it. Big heavy boats full keel boats do it best—but this isn't much help in the end—they only do it easily because they don't heel too much and are often very undercanvased. Driven hard, they round up just like anything else. Again, forget rigs and keels. They don't have anything to do with sheet to tiller self steering.

Some boats will also go along to weather a bit with the helm free and kind of bump and luff to weather in an inefficient manner. Well, this is also natural stability but not too useful. You're noodling along so slow that you're far past maintaining drive, and slowing down. This can as well build a kind of sloppy equilibrium but not a too useful one. I hear someone saying that their boat does better than that—but if it does—you've got a bit of a self–steering system already. Usually that is weight in the rudder, that as the boat heels it tips off to the looward side—thus applying a bit of helm correction. Nifty, I suppose, but inefficient and unnecessary.

Off the wind, now, you've got no natural help from anything. If the boat carried perfectly level helm in perfectly even wind—you might stay relatively put for a bit. But the second the boat gets off course at all the problem flies out of hand. Suppose you turn just a bit to weather. Apparent wind increases—this time creating both more drag and drive—the boat heels too much and you round up even more. The converse, of course, happens if you turn off the wind further. Without applying some correction at the helm—the boat just won't hold a course.

Here's another protest I'm going to hear—probably from someone in a gaff–rigged ketch—who boasts of—like Slocum on Spray—being able to sail off the wind with the helm untended. I don't doubt that in many conditions you might—but that is due primarily to the whopping inefficiencies of the rig and the extra ones you pile on to make the course stability happen. With a ketch one can over–sheet the jib and sheet out the mizzen and achieve something like course stability down wind—as the boat rounds up the jib drags like crazy being oversheeted, the mizzen stalls, the main poops along somewhere in the middle—the center of effort(CE) moves forward and the boat generally wallows off the wind a bit, assuming that there isn't much heel on. If the boat falls off the wind, the jib is blanketed, the main a bit too, but the mizzen is nearly broadside and pulling like crazy in its turn—the CE is way, way aft and the boat rounds up. This kinda works—but at what cost? Wallow wallow wallow. A sheet to tiller system and all sails could draw…

Some might think as well that the trick to getting a boat to steer itself off the wind is to get the CE way out forward. This would be true—if the CE was level with the waterline, but it is not—and any change in course will cause a change in heel—boom, she's gone. A guy can fiddle with a couple of models to prove this to himself if he feels the need. Build a little boat with a stick for a mast—tie a string up at the top and see if you can pull it straight towards you. Play with a couple of keels if you'd like. Move the stick around. Build a heavy one and a light one too. You're going to find that some might work a bit better than others, but unless you're really careful all will yaw all over the place.

So then, the solution: You need to create a system that applies more helm as apparent wind increases—so that if the boat rounds up—the tiller moves to weather and the boat falls off. This is how it works on any point of sail. Simplicity itself.

The obvious beginning: as apparent wind increases, so do the loads on the sheets—thus the sheets are a good place to start to look for something like a meaningful signal that can be applied to the helm. Any control line might work—but the sheets are handy.

The problem: making the signal from the sheets proportional to the signal from—pay attention—HEEL. You are balancing sheet load against heel. Make sure that is understood.

You'll see that somehow there must be a line tied to the end of a tiller, that runs through a little block somehow affixed to one fall of the main sheet pulling a bend in it. The end of this same line goes over to the rail and is made fast somehow—I use a jam cleat. The tiller would be pulled to weather then, doing nothing, so this must be balanced with elastic. Surgical tubing is effective, so are stainless springs—whatever gives the correct tension. You have to vary the amount of bend in the sheet, the amount of purchase in the control line, the stiffness of the elastic, the length of the elastic, etc. for each given boat. Again, you are trying to find a load that varies proportionally to the amount of weather helm the boat has as it progressively heels. You just have to fiddle with it until you figure it out.

You will figure it out. You will find a system that will steer the boat through a range of wind that equates about to a headsail change or a reef—whatever that works out to for your boat. This makes sense, of course, because you are talking a range of HEEL from very little to way too much. One doesn't need to go beyond this amount of range.

Again, there is no kinda working about it. Unless it works, it doesn't. Keep at it. It will work.

PROBLEMS AND WHAT PROBABLY CAUSES THEM

A: Boat keeps rounding up no matter what you do.

> You haven't enough power in the control line. Try putting more bend in the mainsheet by pulling the control line through the jam cleat (or whatever) on the rail.
>
> You might have the elastic improperly adjusted. The end of the elastic will always be VERY near center totally relaxed.

B: Boat keeps falling off no matter what you do:

> You've probably got too much power in the control line. Back off a little bit. Again, the elastic might be adjusted with the helm in the wrong place.

C: Boat just vaguely wanders around.

> You've got a lot of friction, most likely. Either in the rudder post or in the sheet blocks, control blocks, etc. The loads coming off the sheets aren't big enough to overcome the friction. This may cause wide oscillation as well.
>
> Eliminate all the friction you can find and try again. If it still doesn't work, power up the entire system by using a stiffer elastic and putting more bend in the sheet.

D: Things work for a while and then the boat just goes off on a fugue.

This is the most irritating problem—but the most interesting one as well. It is also pretty tough to guess the solution without a clue. You are going to have to translate power into signal. This is done by using a fool's purchase somewhere in the system—in essence making tiller motion out of load in the sheets. I find that a 2 to 1 fool's purchase works for me most of the time—but I'm certain a bigger boat would need much more reduction in power and much more signal strength.

The sheets have got more power than you need by an awful lot. The change in the load as the apparent wind varies is pronounced, but it doesn't look like much—in other words, a sheet can shed quite a bit of load and not move much—that lack of movement is what you need to compensate for by using the fool's purchase and MAGNIFYING that motion.

The answer ISN'T powering up the whole system as it might be to overcome friction. A guy might think that, but it is unlikely that this is the case.

E: Things work, but the boat doesn't handle much in terms of variance in wind speed.

Fiddle with different stiffnesses of elastic. Try as well different lengths. I'd say if the boat won't handle light air but is OK in moderate—the elastic is too stiff. I'd say if the boat is OK in moderate but as the wind builds the boat continues to fall off the wind—I'd say the elastic is too light or perhaps too LONG. You want the elasticity to peak up as the hull induced weather helm does. I don't think the elastic should be any longer than the motion of the tiller would be normally in a course correction. Again, one just has to fiddle until one learns what works.

As a rule of thumb, you're going to need to use stiffer elastic as you encounter heavier sea–states. Off the wind needs stiffer than on the wind.

Elastic really does more to adjust the POWER of the system than anything else.

Ground Tackle and Techniques:

A lot of people have a tough time with the hook. It doesn't need to be so. I'm not really sure that a lot of what gets flipped around in the yacht press is very good information to someone who is cruising in some of the "fringe" ports. Seldom are bottoms ideal, seldom is the depth convenient, and RARELY does one get an opportunity to swing on the publicized 5 to 1 scope. I feel lucky to get a 3 to 1 much of the time. Way too much traffic! Way too many other boats!

There are many different varieties of anchors—we've seen the types. I suppose they're all good, more or less. There really isn't a lot of difference between them when one looks—so why the different types? Because they're HEAVY—the attempts in engineering behind anchors is not so much to make an anchor just hold better, but rather to hold as well but *weigh much less* than some other type. That is a valid concern, for certain, but things are not that simple.

If one looks at a modern, alloy anchor—the specifications for holding are impressive indeed. And, again, if it were only that simple. The problem is not with the holding, it is with getting it SET. The seabed maybe is covered with eelgrass or something else—or may be harder than one thinks, etc. There is no way around this problem except for the initial bite, and this initial bite comes primarily from weight. So, if one wants simple anchoring, get a big heavy hook that looks like it would bite quick and life will be easier. I think there might be a place for a lightweight alloy hook, but not to get away with a *lighter* hook, but rather to get way with a *larger one*. Because of the alloy's light weight it allows me to carry something with awe–inspiring holding power that I wouldn't otherwise—especially in sand. This might be the answer to that desperate and final situation that might just keep me off a beach in a storm. Unlikely, but just maybe…maybe in some distant bay I would need something to kedge me *off* a beach.

As well, we need to realize that most anchors that fail catastrophically DON"T pull out or drag, they BREAK. Imagine that. I then, look askance at anchors that are tricky and funky looking and have lots of moving parts.

What do I use? I've got a pair of 10KG Bruces each on 30 ft of 5/16 chain—300 feet of 5/8 nylon line on that. These have almost never failed to set, nor have the dragged, including the time I rowed one of them out into the bay and stress tested it with my 1971 Bronco, in low range 4 wheel drive and 4.20 gears. If that thing sets—that's it folks. You not break it before you pull it out; if it comes loose it will set again with alacrity. I really trust the Bruce—but among well made anchors it is really just a matter of preference.

How much rode does one need? Depends on where you sail. I carry a 1000 feet. I've been forced to use it all, but I sail in an area where things are often really deep. How much do you need?

If I'm forced to use REALLY short scope—2 to 1 or less—I shackle a 20 lb. mushroom to the head of the chain. Makes for a pretty heavy get up but greatly helps keeping the chain down. The wind has to really howl before I move that around much.

I had at one time another Bruce, a smaller one, which was MUCH more difficult to set. I don't think it makes any sense to own little anchors. They just don't have enough mass to get a good bite and you end up fiddling with them a lot. We've all seen the Friday Night Danforth Show and know what that's all about.

REMEMBER—the two virtues of a good anchorage:

It is protected from hazards under all conditions—this includes other boats that are going to drag. Not too many anchorages are safe from that point of view. In compromise, try to pick your neighbors well. Stay away from boats that are obviously unprepared for a blow—also boats with extreme top–hamper and windage, i.e., powerboats.

It is an anchorage that you can get out of if you need to—meaning when other boats begin to drag, if you simply want to leave to take advantage of a front. As we've said, sailing is the art of riding wind around. Often conditions that can make an anchorage unsafe—say 30 knots of air—can make for spectacular passagemaking conditions, especially in inland waters. The sailor is prepared to take advantage of these conditions and remains ready to set sail and leave...

A lot of times, in moderate weather, you're far safer on a totally exposed beach than in an anchorage.

On Setting a Hook under Sail:

I think it is also good to set a hook at some speed of travel. Mostly you see people motor up, plop the thing, and back up. You've read about boats doing that sort of thing under sail—but there are many books like that where guys gas about traditional sailing techniques and (they read them somewhere) don't know beans about it. While on a large vessel of say 60 feet or so might be able to drop a hook and back under sail reasonably, or a square rigger might—a small sailing yacht isn't likely to generate enough power backing to even pull the chain shot straight let alone set the hook. I like to set the hook sailing at a couple of knots and surge the thing in good and hard. Often times, under the main alone I'll come into a harbor with the rode flaked out on the foredeck ready to run. If it's tight or tricky, I'll lead the chain shot back to the cockpit, but not too often does this prove necessary. If I'm going to anchor, in say, 30 feet, I'll have that ready to go and as I approach where I want to set I'll drop the hook over the side and hold it at about 6 fathoms—keep sailing; as soon as I feel it bump the first time I'll let the whole works go. It pays out with alacrity, I head to the foredeck and as I reach that 4 to 1, I'll take a turn around the bow cleat and surge the boat to a stop. That rode will go taut, the boat will spin around and there I be, set and head to wind. Very slick and fast, and unnerving to everyone else in the anchorage. Don't be panicky about this—three knots is fast but not too fast, as long as one knows how to handle lines there shouldn't be a problem. Likely, even if the hook fouls our fails to set it will still pretty much stop the boat, but not with a surge, so take note, haul the hook aboard, sail out to weather and give it another go. No big deal, you likely just got a big haul of kelp—still, that will spin the boat around. You won't make the beach in any event.

You can do this to weather, as well, if you feel the need. When the rode fetches up you can spin around and try to screw it in the other direction as well. I think a Bruce sets easier with a semi–rotary pull than a straight linear pull anyhow. I can't really validate that but if you look at the flukes you can see why it might. Not a big problem, again, as long as the hook is reasonably heavy.

It is hard to get the feel for a set hook until one has done a bit of anchoring—so I usually suggest a different technique for a novice or myself if I'm expecting a heck of a blow and really want to be certain about my holding..

Sail up to where you want to swing from and drop your primary hook. Do this under the main alone, especially if by oneself, to keep the foredeck clear and so when you let got of the tiller and have the mainsheet sheeted in as far as it will got, your boat will round up and stall nice and easy. Your boat won't do that? Sell it; it's a dog.

Make sure the anchor hits the bottom first and you pay the chain back in a straight line as the boat starts to get sternway. This is the trick, making sure you haven't got wraps around things. If you just dump it in a pile it is quite likely that things will foul up. Better let things tug a bit, You'll start wiggling the hook in. If the wind is really roaring you might just go ahead and accidentally set it. That's OK. We'll confirm the set.

Let's say you feel it starting to grab. Go ahead and pay out a lot of rode in highly antisocial fashion. You aren't going to swing like this so don't sweat it. Pay out to about an 8 to 1. You'll see why in a moment. Don't know how much rode you've paid out? A clever hint—stitch roman numerals on your rode at one fathom intervals. Then you'll know.

At an 8 to 1? Drop the little kedge over the stern, and haul on the bow. Bring our self back up to a 4 to 1. Now you've got a 4 to 1 on both, right?

Take the kedge rode to a sheet winch and haul it bar taut.

Have a beer and watch it for about 15 minutes. Does it stay taut?

Does it slowly, slowly go slack? You're dragging, and if you would have tried this with an engine you never would have known, would you? Feel smug. If you need to, haul the kedge and try again. You'll get a bottom sample when you do; if all you get is a big blob of kelp you'll learn something as well. Move.

Now you've got options. Put the main away while you think about it, as you're going nowhere.

I do, a lot of times, leave both of them down, and I take care to set myself pointing into the direction of wave or wind action. A boat rides very nice like this, but if I've likely got a pretty good current running at some point I might not. Depends. It is often a good idea to keep the bow pointed into the direction of incoming powerboat wakes. Sometimes it's since to pull the kedge and get a couple of chowder clams. At any rate, this technique allows a sailor to really feel a set, and he will sleep better for it. I really recommend making a habit of it, at least until one is comfortable with the anchoring game.

Again, an anchor's hold is primarily determined by its angle of bite to the bottom. This of course is the purpose of scope but can be greatly increased by a heavy chain rode. As I said, if one seldom needs a heavy chain rode but on occasion needs that short scope, a 20 pound or so mushroom anchor can be shackled to the head of the chain rode to act as a sentinel and will greatly increase the holding power of the ground tackle. This is especially useful in an anchorage that is experiencing a good deal of surge, or if one is anchored on an weather shore being set into deeper water.

In areas of deep water and steep shorelines, stern ties are often used. A anchor is let out into deep water and a line is taken ashore to haul the stern toward the beach. The tending angle of the anchor is reasonable even though it invariably on quite short scope, because the angle of the bottom is so great. Again, it is this angle that is all important. Unfortunately, steeply sloping bottoms are often rocky and not the best holding, I personally do not ever feel particularly comfortable with a stern tie although in some areas it is indeed the only option—if the anchor were to drag or come loose from its holding among the rocks in a blow one would be on the beach in seconds.

The Ship's Boat:

As much as one might enjoy sailing, there comes a time when one needs to get ashore. Unless one is minimalist enough to want to swim—one will need a tender of some sort. One small boats the presence of the dingy is a certain inconvenience—and more than an inconvenience is the typical way many people are seen to deal with them, which is a certain hazard.

Let me say that in many cases one might get away with towing a tender, but one does sacrifice a certain amount of speed to the action—perhaps a half a knot? This might not seem like much to one who has the option of motoring into the harbor as the wind dies, but for one *without* that option it seems like a lot to give up, especially when faced with long hours of drifting or rowing. I have towed a dingy in the past, but after having one capsize in a tide rip and create quite a hassle I won't anymore—it becomes a serious problem right quick. I have seen dinghies capsized by powerboat wakes as well. There are places where the instant unexpected presence of a sea–anchor could spell disaster for the yacht.

Some people tow inflatables too, which have less likelihood of catastrophic capsize—but the drag and associated speed loss is yet more pronounced.

Some people carry inflatables on the foredeck—making the foredeck unusable. I suppose if well secured on a powerboat this may be reasonable—but a sailboat needs the foredeck for sailing. I think it looks lubberly and likely impairs weather performance.

I did, for years, carry an inflatable—but I inflated it and stowed it at each usage. This was inconvenient but not as much as one might think, as long as one has a large enough air pump to make the task relatively quick. One can get very large air pumps—as these are used to inflate the large river rafts—that will inflate a small dingy in short order. The deflated inflatable is quite a large bulky package, however, and I can see that on many boats this could be difficult to stow. On an engineless sailboat, however, the old engine compartment often has a great deal of space for this sort of object.

I wasn't happy with the inflatable, but it sufficed. It rowed poorly, for certain, but it was manageable. I wasn't about to put an outboard on the inflatable when the yacht didn't carry an engine. It was clumsy and wet, but I had my hard–shell experience and was done with that. Still, I was certainly looking for a different option.

That option came in the form of a pair of inflatable kayaks. These new inflatable kayaks are not the pool toys one might imagine—they are serious, going places kinds of boats. There are different styles and makes that vary in quality, but they are, by and large, less expensive than the typical yacht inflatable, and to my eye, more durable. They are certainly more fun to paddle around in, and useful, actually for exploring an anchorage. They are not fast like a real sea–kayak is, of course, but they are faster than one would think. I have a pair of singles since a single inflates quickly—five minutes?—most of the time I only need one for rowing out a stern tie or a quick trip ashore. If I need to haul gear, I inflate both—and tow the second one as a barge. If one has crew, it is nice to have a pair of boats for coming and going. They fold into relatively compact bundles—and if the shore was questionable, they could be deflated and carried inland for safe–keeping. The thought of having a tender stolen while ashore always hangs in the back of my mind…

If to be used for rowing out an anchor, what I do is ready the anchor and its chain shot in stops and hang it underneath the kayak. I row out, the nylon rode paying out as I go. When I am where I want to go, I slip the stops and the anchor goes to the bottom. Not a problem, and can be accomplished in conditions that I'd feel endangered in a hard–shell pram.

The inflatable kayaks are EXTREAMLY seaworthy—I would say one in an inflatable kayak and a survival suit could withstand fearsome conditions relatively unscathed—perhaps even surf landings and the like. None of the other options are really provide this ability.

Again, all things are a compromise on a small boat—but I would certainly encourage one to look into inflatable kayaks—there is not much wrong with *this* option.

Foulies:

As a sailor is on occasion required to carry on after the sun and the fun has faded from the sailing—it is important to have really good foul weather gear. Foul weather gear isn't a style issue, nor is it a status statement. In the conditions one needs foul weather gear, it is pretty unlikely that one will have any spectators.

The men who fish for a living in the Gulf of Alaska deal with some of the lousiest weather on the planet—and it isn't a mystery what kind of gear they wear. The requirement isn't just that it be warm and waterproof, but it be durable as well. Foul weather gear with a big tear in it isn't very effective, and if one is actively moving around on a boat it is often easy to wear holes in things quickly.

I advocate the ultra–heavy duty PVC coated fish–boat kind of raingear. There is a difference between brands so it pays to shop. Look for unlined jackets with neoprene cuffs—and good solid, roomy bibs. The urethane coated nylon jackets are initially more stylish and comfortable, but the urethane coating wears quickly. Don't make the mistake of buying lined foulies, as if they get wet, which they will, they are very hard to dry out while underway—the PVC types are pretty much impregnable inside and out, and if one takes a wave down the back of the neck one can go below and change.

Think the same way about foul weather boots. They need to be waterproof, roomy enough to get warm socks inside of, and capable of being dried out.

I think the best underway gear is heavy duty, expedition weight polypropylene long underwear under the foulies. It makes for quick and easy changes and stays dry—quickly protective on deck and quickly comfortable below.

Get a good pair of gloves, but in spite of what the racing people do, never handle lines while wearing them! A terrible bad habit, that…

If the weather is REALLY bad, a quality Type V work suit is the best thing going. Most of these are not too waterproof so wear your foulies over the top of it. This is plenty warm for most any conditions—wear it, you'll enjoy the sailing much more. There is no reason to be cold.

The Handy–Billy:

Every sailboat needs a handy–billy, that large set of blocks used for doing tasks that couldn't be done otherwise. Suppose one needs to get oneself aloft in a bosun's chair to the top of the mast—the handy–billy will do that. Suppose one needs to break a foul anchor loose—the handy–billy will be a huge aid. Any time one needs some very serious grunt—the handy–billy is the key.

I like a couple of fiddle blocks, or a fiddle and a single with a becket for a handy–billy. These should be large blocks—big enough you feel totally comfortable hanging from them. As well, since a good deal of line is going to pass through them—and the only line you've got that is that length is the anchor rode—be sure they're big enough to take that sort of line freely. That will mean blocks with *at least* a 5/8ths of an inch swallow. They won't be cheap, but they don't need to be high speed racing block, so go for heavy duty and not trick. A fishboat marine store will likely be your best source.

So, when you really need power, the handy–billy goes to the load and the fall goes to a sheet winch…with only a 3 to 1 rigged to advantage almost a ton of pulling power comes pretty easily that way. Make sure everything is up to that kind of load if you're really laying on it—know your knots, stay out of the line of possible recoil...

The Skills of a Sailor:

Navigation and Chartwork:

The ability to do good chartwork is seen less and less all the time. Modern electronics have made many of the skills of the navigator obsolete. I think this is really rather sad, as navigational ability was one of the many small things that separated the sailor from the lubber—but many of these skills are still valuable and at the very least should be understood.

I have and do use a GPS unit. It is a tool and an immensely valuable one too. People who accuse me of being a "purist", whatever that means, often wonder why I do. I don't find it surprising at all—navigation has always used tools—if I were going to be a "purist" I'd have to eschew lead lines too. I think that is a little silly, and would be a good way to end up on the beach. I never argue that one should be primitive—elsewise I'd be sailing a dugout canoe. No, only that one's gear should never be a *mask* for the lack of skill—nor should the gear get in the way of the experience. I don't think the question about whether a sailor should use celestial navigation or a GPS unit makes any sense—a sailor should use *both.* Trust neither, use one to confirm the other.

Following this line of thought, I don't, however, have any interest in a chart plotter. The reason for this is that the chart plotter does away with charts—and charts, when chart work is done on them, and notes are made, become very valuable references to local knowledge of where one has been and what one has experienced. To keep these notes on a chart—to make them YOUR charts—to keep a log; these activities greatly increase the amount of knowledge one gains on any passage—the mind learns and remembers by writing down better than anything else—so do so. You'll be well rewarded.

Beside this, the batteries don't go dead on charts. That would indeed be a problem.

I have no interest in writing a text on navigation. This is one thing that the bookshelves are littered with. They are all good and complete, although many are pretty thick and in a lot of ways the techniques described are more useful for piloting a fleet of destroyers than a small boat. What I want to do here, however, is to describe some techniques that I think are quick, practical, and useful for the small boat. To, once again, convey an attitude...

The first would be to establish some sort of navigational protocol. This is a set of data that is always entered every time a chart problem is worked, and every time a log entry is made. A good deal of the time the information entered will just be a generic entry, but none–the–less the act of writing things down means you've thought about it. This in itself is valuable. If you're the type that is writing down conditions, tide, speed of advance, etc., every hour on the hour—you're unlikely to get to surprised by a "sudden change in conditions." This is hardly an inconvenience, it is good seamanship, and truthfully once one is set up to do so it's pretty quick.

Still, one must choose one's personal navigational language. The first thing to choose is whether or not one is going to think in degrees magnetic or not. I think there is hardly a question to it—do all your work in degrees magnetic. The compass obviously thinks in magnetic, the GPS if you use it can generally be set to think in degrees magnetic—your bearings and ranges are going to be in magnetic. About the only time that one is going to encounter a reading that is not explicitly in degrees magnetic is when dealing with the azimuths of celestial bodies—if one chooses to get involved in celestial navigation—but this is easy enough to remember in context because one is really measuring something else altogether...

So then a little chart protocol example. I might write on the chart—

1400—195—5.5

That means to me, 1400 hours, I'm making 195 degrees magnetic, and I'm making 5.5 knots. As these are on the chart, these values are all REAL values off the chart. Meaning, regardless of what I've steered, 195 is what I've found to have made, and 5.5 knots is what I've found to have covered over ground in the last hour. If the spot on the chart is a guess that comes off of dead reckoning or is more or less a guess—mark it as a little x. If it is a better position than that, really a fix, mark it as a little point with a circle around it.

The log, however, is different, and contains a lot more information:

1400			Lat:	48–44.9
CO: 180	CS:180	CMG:195	Lon	122–55.5
SPEED:6.0	VMG:5.5	SOA:5.5		
Observations:	NNE 15 Brising Ebb			

So what have we here? We have the time again, we have the latitude and longitude found off the chart. We have a "course ordered", a "course steered" and a "course made good," which a lot of the time, are not the same thing. The course ordered is what you asked for, if you're not on the helm—some people are perpetually high or low of the mark—it's nice to know. Course steered is what they think they've actually steered—you'll ask, but a lot of the time you can get an admission that they think they were a bit off. Course made good is what actually happened, you got that off the chart. Now you might know if you need to make a correction for the next hour on a couple of different details.

Speed is what you're making through the water, off a chip log or a guess. Velocity made good is what you've actually made over ground—this comes off the chart. Speed of advance is what you're making towards where you want to go—this is the number that gives you an estimated time of arrival and sometimes a bit of a sigh. Of course we're measuring our speed in knots—which is nautical miles per hour, right? And we know that a nautical mile is not a measure of linear distance, right? A nautical mile is one arc minute of a degree of latitude? That way we're not looking for a mileage scale somewhere on the chart, we're picking it up right off the latitude on the side. This becomes really important when you learn celestial navigation...

Observations? This is a bit of a mish–mash and anything you think important. Obviously, what the wind is doing is important, so here it is—the barometer is rising, in my personal shorthand, and we're still on the ebb.

How did you find your position on the chart to begin with? Well, usually, I just look at the GPS. Pretty stupid easy, eh? Of course it is, that's why they built it. There are good tricks, of course, that don't rely on the electronics which are certainly good to know. The first is how to do basic hand bearings. No real trick to this as long as one takes a couple of readings and chooses good objects to take bearings off of in the first place. It is hard to read a hand bearing compass too accurately as a good deal of them are swimmy, though, so know all positions are "likely" positions. Once one has done that, we could check the depth of the water possibly and see if that agrees—this is pretty simple too. If one has a sextant on board, all sorts of neat tricks can be performed and usually with much greater accuracy. By turning a sextant on its side, you can measure the angle between two objects on the horizon, and knowing the bearing to one—you've got a fix just like that and likely a good one as the sextant is mighty accurate. If you can get someone to install a compass like the kind they put in binoculars into the scope on your sextant you can do this all in one operation—very cool, very fast and accurate. If you like fiddling with trigonometry in a seaway, the sextant will read altitudes of objects as well—there are all sorts of tables in Bowditch that will find you where you are.

The trick to navigation is—work neat, work deliberately, do the same thing every time, do it a lot. One gets very attuned to what is going on—even so that one hardly needs to do it anymore—yet this is just the time one must insist on discipline. Consider it a ritual of going to sea, and the likelihood of finding yourself on a reef is much diminished.

One needs to become proficient especially because in sailing a real sailboat, sometimes things don't work out as planned and sometimes one isn't in the harbor at happy hour. Navigation at night makes a lot of people nervous—but I don't think this is very well founded. Navigation at night, in good visibility, at least—is easier for me than in the day time. Navigational lights and aids are much easier for me to see at night, and their watch much easier to recognize than in the day time, when they all seem to appear as fuzzy black dots. It think the reason people think night navigation is difficult is that they ASSUME they know where they are during the day, whether they do or not, and at night it becomes obvious that they don't. In the fog, in the rain, at night—one becomes really pleased with that GPS unit. Traditionally, one must admit, there are times where one just cannot see a thing, and in those conditions traditional boats traditionally ran into things. Navigating by sound and smell are possible, but iffy, and I don't like relying on that sort of thing at all. Learn to do these things—pay attention and think—use all the aids you have available, but let the first line of defense being knowing what you are doing.

Lastly, spend a good deal of time learning to recognize running lights of other vessels. There is no way to do it other than to practice—all of a sudden your eyes will learn the trick and it will never be a problem every again—you'll practically see the boat underneath the lights. Still, unless one does this it is pretty confusing, and just another potential source of terror to add to a midnight adventure already filled with worry…

Speaking of traffic, one of the things people often refer to when advocating an engine is to get out of the way of shipping traffic. This is true, I suppose, but what are were you doing in the traffic lanes to begin with? Why is it that one needs to be there? The shipping lanes are only a little over a mile wide, in a flat calm one could row out of them in twenty minutes—at speed one crosses them in no time at all. Pay attention to the weather! If one is likely to be becalmed—don't be anywhere near the shipping lanes. In the dark, don't be anywhere near the shipping lanes. In poor visibility of any kind, don't be anywhere near the shipping lanes. I make a policy of sailing well outside and in frankly shallow water—you're not going to meet a ship there. If you're becalmed, simply anchor. In the worst weather, and in many places one can find oneself in a row of crab pots that will guide nicely in the absence of any other aid. You'll not meet a freighter here either. Traffic is a hazard like any other that any passage must be planned to avoid.

A quick note about "right of way." Of course a sailing vessel has right of way. A rowing vessel is SOMETIMES referred to as a non-powered vessel and SOMETIMES a powered vessel so it becomes much more awkward. I guess you have right of way when you dip the oars in and not when they're out. I think it is wise, if it can be done—to always enter marinas, etc., with the oars out and ready if for no other reason than they're very effective marks—that is they clearly communicate that you are NOT a powerboat. People often assume that if you sail into a marina you're just practicing—and you've got the motor running. But people are boneheads.

So knowing you've got the right of way, but right of way having no teeth at all and never being enforced—a sailor is put into a bit of a spot. The main difficulty is the many cases of maritime law that insist that if ANY fault is shared in a mishap, then the fault is a fifty–fifty split. This means it is important that you do not share the blame, and are always flawless in your seamanship. Unfortunately, this law also states that if one DOES have the right of way—and one yields it—one shares blame. The privileged vessel MUST STAND ON—this is just as important as the other vessel's duty to yield.

So you're screwed either way. I think it is good practice to use sound signals whenever reasonable—although a lot of people just think you're honking a horn and get pissy—yet one must be certain that one does what is correct. In a lot cases, however, when dealing with traffic of the yachty sort, the best thing to do is just avoid it—if this means waiting an hour or two for the smoke to clear (literally) on a busy evening, so be it.

Back to navigation once more:. It isn't so much important how one plots one's positions and works one's fixes as long as one *does*. On a real sailboat, one must play the navigator in a matter much like one on ocean racer—the key is always to make the best time and sail the most efficient way possible. One cannot be casual about it—cruising in a sailboat is very much like racing, actually. One is always in a race against the turn of the tide, a change in the weather, a storm or a calm. One has to complete one's passages on a certain time schedule much of the time. It is very easy, if one is sloppy in one's navigation, to sail extra distances, to ignore leeway and to have to regain distance to weather than one simply threw out—to not pay attention to the strength and duration of the tidal flow: this all costs time and distance. It makes the likelihood of facing inconvenient circumstances just that more certain. Have a strategy for the passage, sail that strategy, pay attention to how well it is all working out. If you don't, you'll end up drifting around in the dark more often than you'd like, and you'll spend some tiresome hours. If you do—you'll make good time and get a good deal of satisfaction of a job well done.

Lastly, if you feel the need to spend a lot of money on navigational gear, get the absolute best pair of binoculars you can afford. Don't buy them on name, pick them up and look through them, and find the ones that you can see the best through. I think it is awfully hard to beat Fujinon's high–quality line. If you can try them in the dark, you'll really separate the good ones from the bad ones. There is a very big difference in binoculars, and the quality is more or less dependent on price. This is one piece of hardware that is really worth saving money for.

A Word on Knots:

Very few sailing books would be complete without a bit to be said on knots. And I will say only a small amount, because after the publication of Clifford Ashley's "Ashley Book of Knots" all other knot books become a bit silly. The "Ashley Book of Knots" is one of those very few books that ranks with Bowditch as a mandatory source text to have aboard any boat—so I'll refer to it assuming you'll get a copy. Yet, there is a lot of bad information surrounding knots, and I'll try to clarify some of this.

I've fiddled with knots a bit. I'm an experienced rigger, with most of my knowledge involving ships rigged in the late 1700. These ships were entirely fiber rigs, with no wire in them, and knots were the structures that held them together. There are many, many knots to be known, but few of them are any much use to a modern sailor, and fewer yet are much use in modern synthetic line. Still, there are a number that should be demanded of any sailor, but it is not only important to know them—but to also know *where to use them*. Knowing why to use them where one does is critical as well. In this section I am more interested in the why and where than the "how to tie."

I don't think there is any magic to knots except to say this: on any one ship there should only be one knot to be used in each purpose. There is no virtue in the "can't tie a knot, tie a lot" school of securing lines. This is a safety issue as well as a convenience, and also a very effective screen as to the quality of one's potential crew. If one has crew that can't remember to put the right number of turns on a cleat, they've got no business being on a boat.

The Cleat: Tying to a cleat is a knot—and tied improperly it is a problem. The first thing to remember is that the loaded line intersects the base of the cleat at an angle, and thus takes its first turn around the after part of the base of the cleat. This much is critical. After this, we have options. If the cleat is large, and a heavy load is to be expected, a full turn around the cleat before crossing turns are made is prudent.

Most cleats on small boats are not this large, so a half turn us usually made and then crossing turns begin. That is what I do, half–turn around the base, a crossing turn and a reversed locking turn. Neat and compact. Again, whatever one does is fine, as long as it is appropriate, useful, expeditious, and consistent—and never, ever, jams under load. Having to take a half dozen turns off a cleat to release a line is sloppy and dangerous.

The Bowline: Called the king of knots; I'd say it is a knave at best. It is a useful knot but its use is much overrated. A good utility knot for sheets, of course, it has the great disadvantage of not being able to be untied while under load—not a problem? We'll see. It is reasonably secure but not as secure as some and by no means as secure as an eye-splice. A bowline can be tied four ways in stranded line, two ways in braid line—all having slightly different holding properties. I refer you to Ashley's.

When used to secure sheets at the clew of a headsail, they can be tied as to hang up on the shrouds on every tack or to slide over the shrouds. Investigate.

The Clove Hitch: This and its kin would certainly take my vote as the most important knot. Secure, symmetrical, difficult to jam, quick to tie—much closer to the king of knots than any other I can think of. It does, however, have one important but little known property, seldom referred to, that can be readily demonstrated by tying a clove hitch around a winch. Tied one way, it holds, the other, it rolls out freely. Investigate. A clove hitch does not hold on any object that is free to turn.

The Rolling Hitch: This is a clove hitch with an extra turn. I refer you to Ashley's. If the extra hitch is tied so it rides on another, it is called a Midshipman's hitch and is especially secure. Since most all knots tied in synthetic line are less secure than those tied in natural fiber, it is often wise to go for the most secure of the lot.

The Buntline Hitch: This is the most secure hitch I know—and becomes a knife knot under load. It is very compact, strong and secure, and is an excellent upper termination for halyards or any end of a line which much hold a shackle, etc., as it is completely secure yet will not get drawn into a block like a eye splice might. It is again, an application of the clove hitch. I once again, refer you to Ashley's.

The Round Turn and two Half Hitches: This is the best way to secure to an object where heavy loads are to be expected and anticipation of the need to release under load exists. Surprisingly, it is the very close relative of the buntline hitch, and again, another application of the clove hitch. Ashley's once again.

The Square Knot or Reef Knot: For only one purpose, tying in reefs. The proper way to tie is right over left, left over right, with one side slipped and the slip facing UP.

The Round Seizing: a structural binding that will hold nearly kind of knot or turn together with great security. Again, "The Ashley Book of Knots" describes this knot and its many applications.
Any knot seized is a good knot.

Eyesplices: In braid or in three strand, many varieties exist.

My Favorite Bend: Two eyesplices with galvanized thimbles and a solid shackle with the screw moused. Nothing is as secure.

Lastly, a few knots to know for the odd application. All to be found in Ashley's. The carrick bend and its permutations, some favorite stopper knot, the sheet bend, some sort of loop in the bight knot—I prefer the butterfly knot—the constrictor knot, the prussik knot, the venerable marline hitch, and lastly the Tom Fool Knot—which is perhaps the one true traditional knot of the sailor, and the one that appears on the cover of Ashley's, and for good reason…

Again, a sailor needs a good, non–folding, non pointed knife in a sheath and a well shaped, nicely tapered marlinespike...

Rigging:

While we're at it, let's take a look at rigs. There's a lot of nonsense out there about rigs too, but see, rigs are commercial—one can buy a rig and bolt it on thinking its going to work wonders. A bit like the big carburetors the hot rod kids get worked up about. It's a good place to throw money so it does get a lot of hype. You can't get a straight answer in this game but I'm going to try. A sailor who doesn't rely on 'an engine DOES really rely on a rig, for certain, so the question arises...It is good to have confidence in the stick...

We spoke a while back about rig tune for sail shape. We're going to get into that now. This will conversation will be a bit drawn out but it needs to be to answer some questions.

So, what's the right way to rig a boat?

There is no right answer to the answer of what to use for rigging other than this one—if you are going to race, buy rod. That's all there is to it. Your rig will weigh just that much less and the guy with the lightest and most expensive rig will win, at least in the kind of racing people do today. There you have it.

Now if you're going to cruise a sailboat, you've got a lot of questions to ask. What makes a boat sail nicely? What is going to make your rig break? We'll talk about breaking first. The most likely answer is fatigue. Second is corrosion, at least in northern climates. If one goes really hot and salty, these might reverse, but these are your two bugaboos. The traditional way of dealing with both of these problems is simply make all of the pieces meatier so there is just more to rot away, in essence, and this is a legitimate approach as long as one isn't crazy about it. One can easily overbuild a rig, and that isn't necessarily admirable or smart. Have a designated weak link somewhere, please, and try to make it convenient. In the event that you rolled things over or something else like that, you don't want the strength of the rig to exceed that of the hull. It is pretty easy to do that. Wouldn't you rather (if you must choose) break a wire, turnbuckle, flange, etc. or rip out a chainplate as well as a reasonably sized piece of fiberglass? This thought, when dwelt on, brings up that proverbial sinking feeling…

As far as that goes—do your research and do a lot of it. I've rigged boats: I sail my own rig—yeah, I can throw around the formulas too. If you're going to re–rig your boat—do it yourself. You need to know what's up anyway, and this is the way to learn. Let me state this, however, as a bit of a preface: This is one of those areas of engineering where the envelops of error may exceed the designed parameters by quite a lot—so often a guy ends up guessing. And the guy who is often qualified to make the best guess is the guy that knows his boat—he ought to know it. I guess I wouldn't trust anyone who calls themselves a rigger (or any other supposed boat expert) who doesn't spend *at least* as much time on the water *in their own boat* as they do fixing other peoples stuff. You'll see why after hiring a few, then you'll henceforth do all your work yourself. Beware! There are lots of glossy books that sell products—just because one might have a name that's spelled funny and know a magic trick in string or two doesn't mean they necessarily know more than you…

Options?

A) Swaged rig: Forget it. Cheap garbage. That was easy, wasn't it?

B) Stayloks, Norseman fittings, etc. These are the best options for modern wire.

The only real argument against them—and it isn't a good one—is price. It takes next to no skill to build stays with these, and they are hefty. Still, I am nervous about them used at the bottom of stays, where they fill up full of crud and corrosion no matter what one does. Still, a good option if one breaks them down and swaps out the wire every five years—the Stayloks perhaps every ten.

C) Spliced ends: in 7x7 or 7X19 wire.

This is not a bad option on some boats, but don't do it because you think it's going to be cheaper; *not necessarily so.* By the time one has fitted out the mast with custom hardware, bought the jumbo turnbuckles and jumbo thimbles one needs for this construction—one is easily into the price range of Stayloks. Splices are strong, but regardless of the magic values one hears attached to them I don't think it is wise to rate splices at any more than 80% of a wire's breaking strength. Splices in 7x19 are stronger than in 7x7 because the increase in number of strands make for more bearing surface—thus more friction.

I don't think splicing 1x19 is a good idea, although one can. One cannot help but fatigue wire in the process. If I were determined to use 1x19 I'd use a mechanical terminal. Besides, a 1x19 splice is a big lumpy thing and I think they look tacky.

By the way—there are rigging sorts who rave about splices and being something special—but pure hype unless there's a good reason. The good reason that usually exists is that the rigger is getting a good hourly rate—and it takes a lot more time to turn in a splice than screw on a Staylok…

So, for the accounting. What did I do on my boat? 7x7 stainless wire with Stayloks on the top and splices on the bottom. The Stayloks up high are much less likely to corrode and anyway they're hanging upside down so they won't fill up like a bucket. Splices on the bottom where, as my weak link, they're readily inspected. The splice is covered with a leather boot that can be slid up the wire to give things a check over and an occasional washout with a blast of penetrating oil. Some high dollar riggers will tell you to serve stainless—don't: that's stupid. You can't keep the water out. Make sure you don't keep it in.

By the way, you're starting to hear stuff among the cruising set about the virtues of galvanized wire again—*be very wary of this hype.* Sure, galvanized wire is great; it specs out great. Then it rusts, and it's not so great. Now sure, I've too seen the ancient galvanized rigs. Yes, they can last a long time but be sure you know what you're looking at.

First, all of the old galvanized rigs that I've seen were huge and heavily zinced, not the case on small wire, in fact, you're more likely to beat all the zinc off the wire in turning in a splice than keep it. Secondly, the service was huge and heavy and maintained by a crew of moneys that threw gobs of tar around with abandon in the pre–OSHA days. Want to play Jack Tar? I've done plenty of that and let me say that it is only romantic for about 15 minutes and makes a hell of a mess. Service, to work, must be really really good or it's positively detrimental.

But, if you must, don't hire anyone to do it, *do it yourself.* Here's why. Service is really easy to apply, except where it's critical, that is, over the splice itself, where, once again, you've likely ruined the galvanization anyway. No one will care as much as you and here it is really important. The crux is the crotch, of course, and the one at the top, where the water is going to zip right around the thimble and in. Don't use pine tar to slush the works—though people will recommend it—which was originally used not so much for its water keeping ability as its *preservative* quality in hemp. The old service was hemp, eh—you didn't want it to rot. Pine tar is just creosote anyhow, more or less—a little known fact is that it actually absorbs water. No, instead, paint the wire heavily with zinc chromate and then slather it in something like an asphalt shingle adhesive. That will seal it up pretty well. Don't use marline; use nylon net twine which will last a long time once it soaks up that black goo and is kept black.

What a hassle! Yes, of course it's ugly. Now, twice a year, climb, inspect, black down, and repair service. Be up there painting all the obnoxious galvanized hardware. After 5 years, see how much money you've thrown away and next time buy stainless.

Here's the last question and I confess I don't really know how to answer it, because it is very complicated. Anyone who can answer it in a snap doesn't understand the question—a bit like the fellow I once knew that remarked that he had read that Einstein had made the comment that he found the flow of electricity in wires absolutely baffling and couldn't possibly understand it—while this fellow said there wasn't much more to it that just hooking the white wire to one side and the black to the other...The question? How does elasticity affect rig performance? Does the elasticity in the wire make as much difference as touted?

Well, yes and no. Obviously one couldn't build much of a rig out of bungee cord—so we can say elasticity does matter. But how about this for a interesting observation: even 7x19 wire, the stretchiest wire one might use on a rig has a modulus that often exceeds the functional rigidity of the hull. On many boats, when one sees the sag in that headstay, a good part of that is *coming from the hull folding up*, not just stretch in the wire. A scary thought—but demonstrable to anyone with a laser level who is inclined to set the thing up inside and go for a sail. The higher aspect rig one has, the more strain comes on the hull, and the more it flexes and cycles. By the way, fiberglass doesn't really fatigue, it erodes, which is to say, that as it flexes the little glass fibers get broken up and slowly the hull gets weaker. The more it flexes, the more this happens, so it isn't really good to flex a hull all the time; or at least it is good to keep it to a minimum.

Back to the question. With as light as most modern boats are built—you can sit below decks and watch people walk around through the deck above—how many of them can even justify 1x19 wire? Are the hulls just too flimsy to keep significant headstay tension? Is this why many of them go to weather like such dogs in any sort of wind? Had a big high dollar race in my home bay about a while back and it brought down two rigs. Lost five main sails. There are those that said it was blowing 35 knots (I'm not sure that's a justification) but I'd personally be surprised if it broke an honest 30 all day. These were all new boats—they had no excuses other than wimpy gear. What is the real reason that boat designers are evolving towards higher and higher aspect rigs—to compensate for the really crummy rig tension control? Pure fashion? I will not deny that high aspect, light rigs DO make sense in some places—flat water, light air pointing. My 35 year old Renegade, with its ultra low aspect ultra heavy rig and modified full keel, now tacks through 75 degrees in good conditions. I can still make 90 degrees under a storm jib and a reefed main in 35 knots of wind. Very few modern boats could do this—it is frankly rare that I find a boat that points higher. You may not believe this—fine, but when you see me rip by on the weather side you will. I must say, this is perfectly good performance, and any boat designer that is worth his pay knows it. In fact, among high tech, modern boats, I know of no stock displacement hull of the same waterline length that will keep up. I say this not so much out of pride but out of wonder—I would expect modern boats to be *much faster* than they demonstrate themselves to be. Ever sail against a Concordia Yawl? Those suckers go fast, and really point pretty well, and a good modern fancy glass one with a racing interior would only be faster. This is an old, old boat, by design standards. It really makes one wonder why people build anything else.

So before you spend the money on some fancy rig beef up the hull until you are sure that the chain plates aren't moving around. A good deal of your inability to keep the mast in column may be from that. All you need is about a quarter of an inch in deflection to notice, and most boats will give you that and more. A couple of full–length stringers would be a big help. After things are rigid, then start thinking about beefy wire. This is a worthwhile project, and you'll be amazed at how much better the boat handles.

Back on track, stretchy, floppy wire *will* affect sail shape to a certain degree, and if this is uncontrollable, performance suffers. If you do decide to change to stretchier wire for some of the interesting engineering reasons—mostly to use spices and have a more fatigue resistant rig—here is how this will likely affect your sailing performance. First, if you for some reason have a high aspect rig—don't, it's not a coherent system. If you have a low aspect rig, and you go this route, you won't see much of a change in your light air performance—you're not generating enough force to create sag. As the wind builds, you will, and you'll get sag in your headstay that may hurt your sheeting angle, as well as move the draft aft, make the shape baggy, and create a good deal of weather helm. For this reason, I don't recommend stretchy wire for a headstay or a backstay, but there might be good reasons for it athwartships. Some will say that in gusty conditions the elasticity in the shrouds takes a bit of the snap off and one gets a better ride in a chop—besides the heavier weight up there takes the motion off a bit too—which means one's sails stay set better and one might seem faster in these conditions. I'm not sure. I personally lean more towards a rod rig mentality all the time as long as it's well engineered. Experiment: I've now got a rig that self-tunes and as the load comes up it stretches into an idealized shape without lifting a finger. It took me three tries to get to this point, however.

So whatever rig you end up with—assuming it remains a sloop and you to don't freak out and put a junk rig on it—this is how you tune it. A marconi rig is a creature of tension; if the rig isn't tuned properly, which generally means loose or unevenly, you actually increase loads, not decrease them.

Start with the upper shrouds, and snug them up to about a ten percent load. You can either do this with a gauge, which is the best way, or by snugging them up until you can just strum an note into them. That's pretty close. Still, I recommend the gauge, as it is very difficult to work a really nice tune into things without it. 50 pounds makes a difference, or about a half-turn of that turnbuckle, and it is hard to find at times without it.

Again, of course making sure that the mast is in the boat straight up and down, tighten up the upper shrouds. Make them snug. As you tighten up the rest you'll find that these will loosen a bit as the whole boat compresses—you'll begin to see the issue. Then, it is best in my mind to go to the forward lowers and do the same. Then do the after lowers, though these are usually not as tight as the forward lowers. I usually tune to put a little pre-bend in the mast, perhaps an inch and a half of deflection at the top on a 30 foot stick.

Now you grind the forestry and the backstay down in conjunction. The forestay is going to be the tightest wire in the boat, perhaps a 15 percent load. If it is soft, your pointing will suffer. I like to set the main at this point for fiddling with these wires will change my mast bend a bit, and I like to tune some good shape into the main by working the mast bend a bit. You'll find a bit of mast bend makes quite a bit of difference in where the draft in your main will sit, so if you've been having weather helm problems here is a good place to tune some of it out. The backstay usually ends up with a load about the same as the shrouds or even a bit less. If you've got a tunable backstay, this is easy.

After you've done all this, start at the top again. You'll usually find that things are no longer even, but it won't take much to make them so. Sight up the mast track, you should be able to shoot a BB straight up it—it needs to be utterly straight. If you've got real trouble, it's likely because the hull is floppy—we've talked about that—so you might consider doing some glass work to stiffen up the hull in the area of the chain plates.

Lastly, you go sailing and check things out from on tack to the next. It's normal for the lee shrouds to go a bit slack but they shouldn't go sloppy—if so, you'd better snug things up perhaps a turn all around. If nothing helps, you've got deck compression trouble or the like so you'd better look for it.

Tricks of the Trade:

To be a good book on sailing, it needs to be comfortable aboard a boat. A good book on sailing should contain some weighty discussions, but it should also contains some quick morsels—so that on those late nights, after a long hard passage, as the port wine is working into a sailor's blood in some stormy anchorage, the sailor has a thing or two to idylly peruse as he watches for the signs of a dragging anchor….

This is that section of the book.

It also contains a number of interesting tidbits that do not really belong elsewhere.

Anchoring

Heavy anchors always set easier than light ones.

The presence of kelp indicates a good deal of rock and a good deal of current.

Do not ignore the time honored practice of tying to kelp if there is no other option. It is remarkably secure.

Learn a good anchor flake.

Having the anchor rode marked off in Roman numerals stitched in dark twine makes anchoring much easier. Mark in fathoms from the head of the chain shot.

Look for signs of the security of the anchorage—remember that a sandy beach almost always indicates wave action—that driftwood driven high indicates where the waves (and your boat would) go.

If one doesn't secure one's halyards too well, they act as a wind alarm...

If anticipating a blow, put a reef in the main before the blow. Keep all sails bent on and at the ready. One may be forced to leave for the safety of the boat.

Don't trust your depth finder for the final reading of the depth of the bottom in an anchorage. Use a lead line. The depth finder may be reading the top of a deep kelp bed...one needs to know this.

When forced to leave a tight anchorage, realize that the act of hauling in the anchor rode can give one a powerful head start and steerage if done with a good bit of beef. It is nice practice to haul smartly, break the anchor free and be underway at speed all in moments...

Often, if one is alone and faced with an anchor that is tough to break loose, the boat will sail it out. This is done by tacking into the rode, back and forth, to weather of course, and on each tack gaining a little more cable. This action of working back and forth will usually break the anchor out with ease. Some boats will do this more or less by themselves, if the main is sheeted nearly amidships and the helm left free, or even lashed amidships, one can sit on the foredeck and haul the rode easy as it comes—holding it on the deck cleat when it wants to pay out again. As it snubs up, the boat will be put about. One can almost steer in this manner. Again, some boats do this nicely and some don't, but it is certainly worth a try. This technique is especially valuable if one must haul anchor against a stiff headwind.

When the anchor breaks loose, give it a good jerk to be free of the bottom, but it is best to immediately head for the helm leaving the anchor trailing under the boat. Sail on it a bit for deeper water and to be well clear of other boats before finally hauling it aboard and stowing it. You'll find you've likely washed all the mud off of it by this point too.

In an anchorage that you expect might be foul, the use of a tripping line is a good idea and can really save the day. Beware, however, where you use it. If the anchorage is a busy one, and you put a float on the trip line, some bonehead in a powerboat is going to pull it, thinking it is either a mooring or a crab pot. Don't laugh—I'm not joking. Keep an eye on it.

Cooking

Make sure one always has a meal on board that can be prepared in a hurry.

Make sure one's cooking arrangement is secure and functional in a seaway.

It is awfully hard to beat an oven full of baked potatoes as underway food in tough conditions.

Make sure you are prepared for a cooking fire.

Crew

"No crew at all" is better than "bad crew."

Beware of crew sporting deck shoes and sail gloves…

If you ignore that last bit of advice and end up with one of these "heavy swells" aboard—make him (or her) the navigator. That will make them pleased as punch—until you hand them a hand–bearing compass and ask for a running fix and speed of advance. Make sure you're sailing to weather when you do this. Make sure you tack a couple of times while they're working on it. If you can find really rough water, that's better yet.

It is unlikely that any crew member will know the boat as well as you. Make sure that the crew is trained as much as possible. Insist on certain ways to secure lines, etc., as these things matter on a boat that sails. If a crew member is casual about these things or uninterested, take note. It is a good idea to find other crew.

A good skipper has trained his crew so well that he need give no commands…he certainly never need yell.

People on the foredeck are generally slow to learn that if they yell while facing forward they can't be heard.

Know the difference between crew and *passengers*…

Line handling

Make sure one knows what a *fair lead* is on a line and why it is important. Foul leads indeed jam cleats, and this is a serious safety issue.

If anchor rodes have eyes spliced into each end—with good solid thimbles—it makes the job of bending them together with ultimate security as easy as a galvanized shackle

Always mouse a shackle!

For quick and simple exits from a dock or a mooring single-handed—consider the use of a toggle. A toggle is a wooden fid, perhaps a foot long, tapered, with a light line attacked to one end. If a mooring line with a generous loop in the end is taken to the ring on a mooring—the loop can be passed through the ring, and the a bight from the standing part of the line passed through the end of the loop. If the toggle is inserted in this loop in the bight, and tension applied to the line, the bight will draw up, pinning both legs of the loop against the toggle—and will hold securely. If the line to the toggle is given a jerk, all will spill and the line will release. Of course this can be easily done from the cockpit of the boat and is a nice way to maintain control while shorthanded. Of course, always again watch for the fair lead...

Consider a toggle with a line lead to the cockpit for dropping the anchor if you're shorthanded. It might make things on some boats much more simple.

The key to coiling line is in the lay. Modern three strand line is coiled in a clockwise fashion, with a slight twist imparted in each turn to keep each turn of the coil laying fair. Braid line has no lay and has a tendency to generate twists if coiled—so it is often coiled with reversing turns—much more of a hassle. Fortunately, on modern boats, we seldom see long lines anymore so this is less of an issue than it once was in the days of tall ships with huge multi–sheave blocks. Perhaps the only place where coiling a line remains critical is in the use of a heaving line—which every sailboat should have and at the ready. A heaving line is best thrown with half a coil in each hand—and it is imperative that both coils be *flawless*...

Quarter inch three strand spun dacron makes a nice heaving line. Choosing a reasonable weight that is comfortable for the monkey's fist in the end, one should be able to throw a heaving line at least a hundred feet.

Navigation

Learn to judge distance by eye. This can be done by learning one's personal eye resolution. For example, one may be able to see, buildings at several miles, but make out individual windows at one mile, and further benchmark details at less than that. This is a very useful skill if deliberately developed. It is often very difficult to judge distance across ·water, and all tools one can learn are of good use.

As well, different colors of light generally have different ranges in different conditions—with experience this can be used to judge distance too.

Don't ignore one's sense of smell. Often reefs, especially, can be smelled a good distance to looward.

When taking bearings, of course it is wise to choose objects that have as many degrees difference as possible—for example, three bearings 120 degrees apart would be ideal. Practically speaking, however, this is seldom the case, but in consideration one must choose as close to the ideal as possible to diminish the envelope of error.

Pay good attention to reciprocal tacks, and be honest about what one is making good to weather on each. Hopefully it will be 90 degrees or better, but don't expect a lot better, especially if a sea is running. Looking at reciprocal compass headings is no good for this, obviously, at it doesn't give one's course over ground, just the direction the boat's bow is pointing, and a boat can look like it points high and is quite weatherly but actually is making a good deal of leeway.

When you get involved in celestial navigation—be careful how you learn it. A great deal of the celestial navigation books available are written with a strong naval tradition behind them, and some of the techniques taught are not so applicable for the small boat. First and foremost the large tables, HO 229 and 249, often used—are touted for their convenience, ignoring the fact that they are huge books and take up a great deal of space, as well as being expensive. It should be well noted that the only reason one might want to use HO 229 on a small boat is because one is very sloppy with one's math, as there are several fewer entries. Otherwise, the short tables are very nearly as accurate, and practically certainly so—though again, they require a few more table entries. Yet I feel the advantage of having a short table perhaps 60 pages in length is a major advantage, and I would heartily recommend it. I agree with others that HO 208 is one of the best to be found.

Remember that a celestial line of position can be combined with any other type of navigational data—say a sighted magnetic bearing, to provide a fix—but remember to account for declination.

Sailhandling

On many boats of about 30 feet in length, rather than sheeting a mainsail in and across in execution of a gibe, it is easier to grab one fall in the middle of the mainsheet and pull it like a bow—this accomplishes the same thing but leaves lines coiled and the end on the cleat. It is often faster as well.

When furling the main, using the mainsheet to secure it does double duty. If one daisy–chains around the sail—this technique called "Swedish furling"—the main and the main sheet are secure but ready for use in a snap.

The "racers" technique of flaking a sail on the boom is reasonable for harbors—but a sailor needs a sea furl that is secure and will not hold water. The best way to do this is to grab the leech of the main at perhaps the first reef point, and pulling away from the boom. This forms a pocket which is in essence all the cloth of the first reef. The rest of the sail is tucked into this pocket, and the whole works neatly rolled up on top of the boom and secured.

Never stand on a sail.

Never pull a sail down by its leech.

Never let a sail flog.

Try to never fold a sail the same way twice. Modern cloth is vulnerable to creasing and fatigue.

I personally believe that tell–tales on sails are a bad idea. I don't like wind direction indicators either. The reason for this is simple—they are unnecessary, on can learn to trim sails effectively without them and should. Besides this, the presence of tell–tales often encourage the bad habit of staring at them, when a sailor, especially a single–handing one, has better things to be looking for. A boat can be sailed effectively entirely by feel—and this should be learned. Lastly, the reality is that if one becomes dependent on tell–tales and the like to steer a good course, what does one do when sailing at night? One needs to be able to anticipate an accidental gibe by feel, once again, or night sailing may be unnecessarily dangerous.

At times it becomes useful to be able to make a quick headsail change. Foil headstays an the like are indeed quick, but of in my opinion a bit fragile for a cruising boat. Twin headstays, as one used to see on older boats, seem to me to be heavy and clumsy. Actually, with good practiced hands, a relatively quick headsail change can be made in the following manner with little gear. The trick is to have the second headsail bent on as much as possible before the first is lowered, and thus be without a headsail for as short a time as one can. Obviously this concern is more important when sizing up a sail than sizing down—as if one is overcanvased dropping a jib altogether is of little concern. What one does is to release perhaps the lowest piston hank on the working jib, and to hank the sail to be hoisted onto the forestay in this space. Then the halyard is lowered and shifted to the new sail, the hanks on the dowsed sail are removed quickly, and the new headsail is hoisted. It is useful as well to have a pair of shackles at the tack for this maneuver. A headsail can change can probably be made in a third of the time it would take otherwise in this manner.

A shackle on the clew of a jib sheet is fast and convenient but a good way to loose teeth…it is best for each jib to have its own set of sheets and for them to be spliced on. Splices are far less likely to hang on the shrouds than anything else to use to attach to the clew.

Tactical Sailing

Always plan for a destination and plan for an alternative if things don't work out.

When faced with entering a new harbor for the first time, try to time one's passage so that one can do so under oars in a near calm. If this means one must anchor outside the breakwater for a couple of hours—so be it. This is seamanship.

In sailing tidal races, unless the wind is strong and constant—try to sail them to weather, at the slack, with the current filling in behind. This way as the current fills in, apparent wind increases and one maintains good control. Otherwise, one risks becoming becalmed and loosing steerage as the current and wind move in the same direction. This effect is more pronounced than one might think.

Again, favor the starboard tack unless there is a good reason not to. That reason might be sea–state, as typically one tack will be more contrary to the waves than another.

Remember than any place you can touch bottom is an anchorage in a flat calm.

Anyplace you can anchor to avoid loosing way is reasonable too.

A twenty knot blow in January with driving rain may carry nearly twice the *force* of a twenty knot blow in July. The force of the wind is dependant on speed, but of course also greatly dependant on density of the fluid medium—thus temperature, humidity, and carried precipitation.

Speaking of force—as sailors are more concerned with force than with velocity—the traditional Beaufort Wind scale still does make far more sense than describing wind speed in knots. Note that each force is described by a range of velocity that manifests a given effect—this effect is the expression of force. Thus, I believe it good habit to use the Beaufort scale although many find it a bit archaic and pretentious—the fact is, for the uses of a sailor, it remains the most *accurate*.

When crossing a strait, or a set of traffic lanes, do so more or less perpendicularly to avoid spending any more time in the hazardous middle than necessary.

Tide

It has been suggested that one can determine the likely duration of slack water by taking the maximum anticipated velocity of the tide in knots, and by dividing this number into sixty, a result is derived in minutes that corresponds to the duration of the slack. That is to say, for example, a 6 knot current gives a 10 minute slack.

I would suggest that any time you've got in excess of a 4 knot current—you're not going to have a slack water at all.

The maximum speed of a current is not necessarily dependent on its position within a tide cycle, which is to say that the current cycles may be asymmetrical. Full flood or ebb is not necessarily at mid–tide.

Strong winds can accelerate or stop tidal flow. For example, a strong on–shore wind may delay the onset of an ebb—the resultant ebb being significantly stronger than normal.

The change in tide often can spell a change in weather.

Current is usually least near shore, with the exceptions of spits and points which accelerate current.

Underway

A ship is only as safe as it is ship–shape. Keep all lines coiled and ready to run.

Remember that unless it is specifically ballast, all weight on a boat slows it down. Weight high and in the ends is the worst.

Weight on board makes a boat gives a boat more *initial stability* but less *ultimate stability*. Which is to say that weight makes a boat more resistant to heel but more likely to capsize.

People say that loading a boat helps it pound through waves and makes it faster. This has been proven again and again not to be true. While it is true that heavier boat does slow less while encountering each wave, it also accelerates less each time it gets through it. No, loading a boat only makes it *slower*.

Always know both the tide and weather forecast for every sail. Always have the proper chart at the ready.

Oil lamps make excellent interior running lamps at night, as they draw no electrical power and effect one's night vision minimally if kept low.

Anything that can come adrift certainly will. Practice good stowage.

Make sure the bilge is kept clean. A dirty bilge can sink a boat.

All through–hulls should have real damage control plugs lashed to them and at the ready. In the case of a flooding, one only has moments to get it under control. Once the cabin sole is awash, most survivors report that they could no longer determine the source of the flooding…

Keep a large, handheld spot–light on the boat and ready. It will draw far more attention than running lights will.

If underway at night, and one finds oneself in a situation where one must wait for conditions to change to make a harbor entry, etc., because of bad visibility—a good place to sail to kill the hours is in the immediate proximity of a large navigational buoy. Certainly, sailing around and around a buoy for hours is tedious, for certain, but it is a very safe place to be and eliminates a good deal of worries. One knows that all large ship traffic will be watching for the buoy, and while they might not notice you they will notice *it,* and will avoid the general area. Likewise, being a hundred yards from a navigational buoy makes one's personal navigational problems relatively simple…

Always have a couple of gaskets at the ready for use in securing sails and anything else that might want to come adrift. A half–dozen pieces of $^3/_4$ inch nylon webbing are convenient. One should always have at least one of these in a pocket, especially when heading for the foredeck.

Some Sea Stories:

T he following are a few selected accounts of some memorable voyages in sailboats—selected because they convey the atmosphere and attitude of the sorts of situations sailors encounter—perhaps one will hear an encouraging call in these accounts…

A quick trip on RENEGADE.

So at 1 in the morning I hear a knock at my hatch. Since bad folk rarely knock the shotgun stays where it sleeps and I get up and peek out the hatch. Well, hell! A sailor buddy of mine back in town after being off in the Sea of Cortez for the last eight months. Coffee's on: lots of sea stories follow—some of which were even likely true. We decide to go sailing, visit another friend in a port about 100 miles to the south in Port Townsend—I haven't got any work lined up next week so we'll leave on the ebb first thing in the morning. The barometer is high; it has been blowing northwesterlies for the last three days—there are rumors of a depression working up the coast. Sounds like a great sail. Four or five days, reach down and reach back.

We leave in the morning. It is absolutely flat calm so we row out of the harbor. We are not far out when a light southerly comes up. Not a real great sign—with a high barometer a southerly in our area can only mean local effect stuff—but it is on the nose and with the 180 genoa set we're actually making good time on the flat water. We decide to hug the gradient of a large mud bay on our way in case the wind totally dies—when can just drop the hook right there. Everything is an anchorage in a flat calm.

The wind dies. It is just a tad before noon, and the current is still taking us in the direction we want to go, so we simply break out lunch and the stereo and drift along. After about eight cans of beer the expected northerly starts to fill in and we take off. After about an hour we've got a decision to make—tide is starting to change. We look at the charts and it's not going to be a big run-off. We can either take a longer route and face less current or a shorter route with more—at any rate we want to be in harbor in Anacortes an hour before sunset because the wind nearly always dies. We opt for the short route and pile on the sail; we are determined to make time while the wind holds. It turns out to be a good choice; the wind holds nicely and we bomb into the harbor several hours sooner than we thought.

We leave next morning on the ebb again. We've got a good northerly as soon as we're underway. Tack through a narrow channel with wildly variable winds and out into the Straits of Juan de Fuca. Wind starts to fall light about noon again, and our speed is greatly reduced. We desperately want to make Admiralty Inlet before the late ebb—it is going to be a big one and there is no way we'll hold against it in this air. We claw our way along making as much way as possible, even rowing a bit from time to time, and we make the Inlet just as the tide turns. We've got about five knots of air, we've got a dead down wind approach, and the current is dead in our face and building. Looks pretty bad.

Desperate strategies evolve. We'll see how far we can get and if we start to loose way we'll turn around and hang for the night in a small mud bay about six miles off. It will be a long night, but that's playing sailor. We notice that there is a bit of a lift off the south point—it's pretty shallow over there but deep enough, especially at our rate of speed. We sneak over there and actually discover bit of a back eddy—we're actually now making 2 knots over ground! Will it hold? Don't know—it's pretty small, and we can see the ebb really starting to pick up only a hundred yards to the north. We scope it out with the glasses. Well, it sure looks like it holds around the point—there is a lane of glassy water all the way around the corner. We don't think it's flat (windwise) there because we would anticipate the wind to actually pick up a bit due to the topography. We guess the glassy flatness can only be due to the water moving in the same direction as the wind—hot dog! We're going for it. Yes, the water does get a bit thin but we've careful, and we sneak around Point Wilson at sunset and into har-

bor at Port Townsend with the feeling we cheated things a bit. A useful note is entered into the log.

We fiddle around in town for a day. The front from the south has deepened a bit and is expected in the morning. Small craft advisory southerlies posted. We're going to make great time heading back north.

We leave in the morning on the ebb again. Very little wind, actually, but the barometer has fallen—though not as much as I would have expected. We whip out through the Inlet on a heavy ebb into a sloppy low swell running in from the Pacific. Breakers out over there; I believe we'll avoid that. Yup, it's blowing out there somewhere. A couple of hours later we've still got very little wind, and we've only made but a couple of miles to the north due to the lumpy sea state. Barometer is falling. I don't like it a bit.

Neither did NOAA. They've got a gale warning posted now for 40–knot westerlies.

Aw, Damn! Sounds like we get to play sailor after all. We make a quick strategy pow–wow. Our first priority it to be out of the Straits before 40 knots shows up. Pretty hefty tides all day today and with the typical 2 knot currents it's going to be LUMPY. We harden up sails and blast off in a northwesterly direction: it isn't where we want to go but there are a couple of good bays up there that we can hide in if it comes to it. Now that we're on the wind we're making good time. If the wind comes up we want all of the extra distance to weather we can get in case we have to fall of and run under my spitfire jib—even in that case we ought to be able to find a place to hide.

Wind builds. We are driving the boat. We are making excellent time. Can you say performance? Can you say performance? Wind is clocking from Southwest to West as we head on north. Actually, that's becoming close to ideal. We are really hauling ass now, running in the high sevens in a four–foot slop. I don't like it and I've got the boom preventer really tacked down, but this is one of those times when driving a boat hard is prudent seamanship.

We blast in around the corner, into the lee of the islands. The wind builds; the slop moderates. We're now heading north on the full flood. GPS is reading and holding 9 knots over ground. The main gets a reef and now the helm balance is reasonable. We blast into Anacortes, it's about 3 in the afternoon. It's blowing a very irregular 25 and all over big powerboats are running for shelter. There is no way I'm going to sail into the harbor right now. We think for a moment, gybe, and point the bow north for Bellingham with Van Halen thumping the speakers.

It is a sloppy ride through the islands. We get to see everything from a flat calm to thirty knots in gusts and we have a regular sail change drill. We get into Bellingham before dark and it is still blowing pretty solid in Bellingham Bay. I'm not too keen about running into the boat harbor with the lump that is running across the entrance, and I'm going to have a hell of a time keeping the speed off once inside. We sail up, check it out, don't like it, and stand off. I drop the headsail. We noodle around off the waterfront waiting in hopes of the wind to die at dark—else we'll have to find a spot to hide for the night. I make supper—the wind moderates a bit—though not as much as I'd like and we come jamming on into the marina under bare poles. I back water hard with the sweeps and crab my way down the pier to my slip. Pause for a moment, and we're home. Gosh, that was easier than I thought it would be.

Put stuff away. Have a beer. Have another. That's sailing.

Down the coast in PHOCA:

In May 2000, having owned and sailed the 28–foot Atkin designed ketch, Phoca, for five years, I decided to remove the diesel engine. We planned to sail north into British Columbia, then head down the west coast to Baja and the Gulf of California. I suppose I had entertained the notion of removing the engine for quite some time, feeling that it would give greater storage of water, tools, and food, increase her speed and beauty as a sail craft, and test my sailing and seamanship skills in the "sink–or–swim" way. Some people had dark predictions about our upcoming trip, but there were a few encouraging adventurers whose voices rose above the backdrop of naysayers. These people had stories I wanted to listen to, and their knowledge through experience I integrated into my own. My sailing partner and girlfriend Djuna and I have come to feel that that the fun–less moments (which can last from minutes to days) of engineless sailing are balanced by the more fun ones (which can last from minutes to days).

After a 14–day nonstop passage from Neah Bay, Washington to Newport Beach, California, and followed by two months of living in the heart of materialistic and status–seeking Southern California, Djuna and I were ready to make southerly tracks. Thankfully, things had worked out well for us; we had found work, kept our meager stash of money intact, made some minor improvements to our little floating world, and had met some great people. The hurricane season was ending and Djuna had hinted that she might lose it mentally if we did not leave soon.

We had decided that our first landfall in Mexico should be Isla Guadalupe. This island lies about 180 miles offshore Northern Baja, and is roughly 375 miles, as the crow flies, from Newport Beach. I had dreamt of seeing this island for myself ever since I had read Lin and Larry Pardey's stories of adventures in Saraphin, and there was definite appeal in sailing to a small, offshore, volcanic island where elephant seal breeding colonies exist—as well as the Great White sharks that prey on them. We knew that the "anchorages" on the island were sketchy at best and that if the weather was iffy, we might not even stop, opting to sail on towards Isla Cedros

It was 1200 or so, November 18th, and our friends had said they were coming to say goodbye before noon. We had spent the previous evening preparing for sea and cramming tools, sails, and lots of water in various containers into what had once been the engine compartment. We did a good job of it too, for we had learned our lesson about "loose items" after being becalmed on our previous passage…Unfortunately, our friends were nowhere in sight and I was antsy to get out of the harbor and across 12 miles of one of the busiest shipping lanes on the West Coast before the wind died in the evening. We bade them a mental farewell and pivoted the boat 180 degrees with lines to mooring buoys. Once pointed downwind, we *raised some sail and let go. A little improvised slaloming and we were in the clear and headed for the harbor entrance two miles away.*

Once clear of the breakwater and we steered west–southwest, beginning to feel the Northwest swell and wind. We were scooting along, on a beam reach under full sail, with our self–steering gear working well. The coast was clear (so to speak) for ships, so I went below to do some last–minute stowing and grab a snack and a couple of bottles of water to ensure that we would drink enough over the next day. Both of us were too excited to sleep, ut I went below anyway to try to rest before nightfall, leaving Djuna to be captain. By nightfall we were 8 miles off the southeast end of Catalina Island and experiencing very little wind. I was starting to feel seasick—no surprise since I suffer from that curse—but knew from past experience that no matter how horrible I felt, so far I'd been able to do anything which needed doing, as had Djuna.

The night was calm, but after a little while I could hear approaching wind from the land. Sure enough, about 20 minutes later a light wind was blowing from the Northeast and we were moving though the water once again. I silently gave thanks to the Wind God for sparing us the discomfort of wallowing in the swells and for giving us our mobility. I had just settled into a cozy area of the cockpit when I was startled by something out of the corner of my eye. My pulse slowed when I recognized the strange orange shape of the moon rising from behind the mountains of the coast which was to be our last glimpse of land for the next three days.

Day 2 dawned high overcast with a light northwest wind. Too light for our liking, in fact. That day passed by, us repeatedly raising and lowering the drifter in exchange for the light–wind jib—sometimes taking down all sail to save our ears and sails from the slatting in the much larger swell. Preparing myself a lunch of tuna, salad dressing, and instant mashed potatoes (I highly recommend these) I wished the wind would increase. Djuna and I traded watches in what felt like a natural rhythm of 4–6 hours and about 3 hours at night. This schedule seemed to afford us enough sleep, but with so many sail changes we were up a time or two on our off–watch. However, that night I had my first restful sleep while Djuna kept and eye on things out in the cockpit, listening to tunes on the Walkman that were written in a world much different from what was now ours.

Day 3 was celebrated by the return of my appetite, and the absence of nausea. We paid our dues and from now on our lives at sea would be much more comfortable. The sky was still a high gray overcast, with a building northwest swell, we were sailing under light–air jib, whisker–poled out to one side and drifter sheeted to the end of the main boom on the other side, our preferred downwind combination for light air. I checked the barometer regularly, wanting wind yet sighing with relief at the needle's reluctance to move. At one point in the afternoon I happened to glance aloft and notice (to my dismay) that the leech of the drifter had flopped over on a roll and had hooked itself into the bronze clip which serves as the upper end of the jib downhaul. As the boat rolled the other way, the drifter inflated and ripped along the leech. I could see what looked like two feet of tear so it must not have been hooked for long, but I wanted to save the sail from as much damage as we could. Djuna was down below sleeping and I realized that to solve the problem, we needed to drop both sails simultaneously, or more ripping would occur. I yelled for Djuna to "come up ASAP! Skip the foulies, Skip the harness! Just get up here! The longer you wait the more it will rip!" She woke up about half way though my ranting, unsure of who I was yelling at. Once she came up we got the drifter down with a little more damage, and Djuna volunteered to resew about 3 feet of the leech. She was now standing on sea legs. Without the drifter up, our progress was halved at least, and I will stress to any prospective engineless sailor my opinions on the importance of large area, light–wind sails…

The rest of the day passed uneventfully. We hadn't even seen a distant ship, let alone any marine life since our first night, so were feeling a bit lonely, and the monotone of the gray of the sky had an ominous feel to me. "Oh well," I thought, "If anything's gonna happen, it's going happen." That evening we were about sixty miles north of Punta Del Norte, the north end of the island, and after an uneventful night with the same light air exercises, Day 4 found us about 25 miles off. We knew that soon we should be able to see the island; it rises out of the water to a height of 4000 feet in about half a mile of horizontal distance. We kept moving forward, and we kept not seeing it. Finally, and about 10:00 we spotted a dark shape up in the clouds, and realized that this was Isla Guadalupe. Within minutes, the island shed its clouds and it appeared in its entirety, looking larger than we had anticipated.

Our first island landfall had me feeling awed yet wary. The island resembled a huge dragon rising out of the ocean; with a volcanic spine of a central ridge, slopes cut with more weathering–resistant dikes and sills, and seemed to communicate a message to keep away. The stationary lenticular cloud which clung to the main ridge was visible as this strange conveyor—clouds appearing on the leading edge of the lens, blowing across the ridge, then disappearing at a precise line in the sky. The sound of the huge surf four miles away definitely added to the vibe.

A distinct edge of the cloud–cover which had been our company for the last three days was visible further to the west, moving south, and soon it was hot and sunny, the wind completely gone. We broke out the 11 foot sweeps we call our "two–stroke" or "sympathy sticks" depending on the situation, and began rowing the last two miles towards our anchorage. We traded off for the next hour, and were closing in when fishermen in pangas started coming in to their little camp which we were hoping to anchor near. One of them, noticing our less common method of travel, came alongside to ask if everything was ok. We conversed in English and Spanish (their English was better than my Spanish) and they introduced themselves. They seemed exited about having visitors and asked if we were hungry. We were, so they grabbed three lobster from their coolers and gave them to us. They asked for nothing in return but we had some beer and soda—none of it cold, of course, but they were as pleased as us with tepid soda, so we chatted while sipping our drinks. They warned us not to swim or dive because of the sharks, invited us to come fishing with them the next day, to come ashore and shoot a goat with a shotgun they would be glad to loan us, and many other things. They made us feel quite welcome but we declined, wanting to rest and clean up, thinking we could talk in the morning.

Having eaten a large meal, Djuna and I finally relaxed into the awesomeness of the scene surrounding us. It felt like we were looking straight up to the top of the ridge 4000 feet above, and the ever–present lenticular cloud we were now viewing from behind and below—though it continued to disappear at a distinct line far above our heads. I was very psyched, energized, and glad we had decided to come see this place. Soon it was dark, so we broke out the soap and bucket, got clean, then made up the 2–person berth. Snuggled into our warm little be I cultivated the dream of a leisurely .wake–up after a full night of worry–free sleep. I lay awake listening to the diversity of sounds bellowed and belched with abandon from one of the many seals ashore, underlain by the sound (transmitted though the hull) of gravel and cobbles being swept up and down the beach slope by the refracted swells. That sound was a bit unnerving…

At 0227 (exactly!) we were both awakened by the sound of chain on the bottom and the whistle hum of wind blasting over us. We had read and heard about the williwaws that which the area hosted form time to time, so we knew what we could be in for. We quickly dressed (with reluctance) and readied PHOCA for sail, then went back below for sleep (if possible) fully clothed until first light.

Three and a half hours later, we were ready to go. The gusts were about thirty knots, some maybe higher, and we didn't like the way that sometimes they would blow about 45 to 90 degrees off the shore, and at other times it was more like 20 degrees to parallel. We wanted to get the anchor off the bottom while falling off, headed away from shore. I believe we did, and I remember the feeling of relief tinged with wistfulness that grew as we fell off, never having touched the island.

It was a beautiful day, the sea was alive, and if this wind held, we could make Isla San Benito, 150 miles distant, by the next morning…

Matt Nelson

Getting one's sealegs:

I got into sailing just a couple of years ago. Why, I'm not sure, but it seemed like the thing to do. None–the–less, I bought my first boat—had a friend tear the engine out of it—and I was ready to learn what to do.

No, I didn't know a thing about sailing when I bought the boat, and I didn't know how to sail when I had the engine tore out. The only other boat I had ever been on, however, was owned by a friend of mine, it had no engine and we went places in it just fine. I sure liked the idea of a sailboat without an engine. I liked having lots of room for stowing things. I liked how the engineless boat was so much faster than most all the other boats we'd see. I also really wanted to learn how to sail, and while I didn't know, I could certainly tell that nobody else did either. It was a circus every marina we got into. My buddy knew how to sail, that was clear, and I understood that came from not so much being more talented but rather really having done it.

So, yeah, I had the engine tore out. I bought some oars. I've never even been on a boat with an engine in it.

I took my first cruise in Yggdrassil, my Albin Vega, last summer. I hadn't ever been out of the local bay before, and I needed to learn some things. I had my sailing buddy along for crew so I wasn't too worried, but it was good to use my boat and see what it was capable of. I had learned a lot so far, sailing in the bay and in and out of the harbor, but there are decisions and issues one faces only by making long trips. This would be the first long trip.

We left Bellingham early in the morning, rowing out of the harbor in the morning calm. It was supposed to blow pretty well that day and we wanted to make a good deal of time north, but it was also supposed to blow hard enough that we could have gotten stuck in the marina so we left. Once we got outside, though, there was a little wind and we took off at a couple of knots. We had Hale's Passage to deal with about 7 miles to the south, and we needed to hit that on the flood tide. It looked like we'd be a little late and more into the flood than we'd like, as we were hoping to ride it north, but one doesn't always get to choose what the weather is.

A couple of hours later we were still only making a couple of knots, the wind hadn't filled in. My buddy didn't like it, we could make it through Hale's but we'd end up in the straits on the north end and in the shipping lanes. We didn't want to drift around there. There was a small bay at the south end of the passage that we thought we'd anchor in if the wind didn't fill in. The wind didn't fill in. We sailed into the bay and anchored close to the entrance to make it easy to leave once we finally got breeze.

No wind all day. We sat in the sunshine, listened to the stereo, and enjoyed the solitude.

Until about six o'clock, that is. All of a sudden the bay started filling up with other boats. They anchored everywhere. As the bay got more and more crowded, people anchored on shorter and shorter scope to be "considerate" of each other. Some fat guy came out and played the bagpipes. It was weird.

My buddy didn't like it. The weather, that is—he didn't like the bag-pipes either. We'd been watching the barometer and it was still falling but no wind. We figured it was going to show up at some point or another and that when it did, it would show up quick. We hoped it would be next morning.

Just in case we put a reef in the main, got everything stowed, and had everything ready to make sail at a moment's notice.

Good thing too, the wind came up at midnight with a howl. Halyards were slapping, motors were running instantly—you could see people run-ning around in waving flashlights and hoping they weren't dragging. Boats were starting to swing around and bump into each other. It was time for us to jimmy out of there.

We did. We set the main, hauled the hook like hell—five shorts on the horn and a wave at the spotlights across the exit (there was a reef out there we wanted to avoid) and we were gone in a heartbeat. When we got out-side the entrance of the bay the wind was really rocking, probably 30 knots, and we decided we'd sail on under the reefed main alone to keep the speed down a bit. Visibility was good and we stormed north in the dark trailing huge plumes of phosphoresce behind us.

A few hours later we were miles away, having sailing into a nice anchorage at dawn, the sails stowed, we had a real breakfast, and spent the day fiddling around and catching up on sleep.

The next morning we were hoping to head north to Vancouver. There was supposed to be some wind but not a lot. We had traffic lanes to thing about and pretty big tides. We weren't really sure we wanted to go but finally got antsy and left. Once we got away from the island and into the flood stream the wind all but died. We were able to make way but only a knot or two under the huge abomination spinnaker. The weather was warm and nice and it wasn't too bad. We got across the traffic lanes as quickly as possible and sailed in the shallow water of the Fraisier River delta with the idea that if the wind died we'd just anchor right there amidst the crab pots. We had done that before. Not a protected anchorage, obviously, but if the wind came up you left.

The wind died. We anchored. A light wind came up in the early morning but only enough to stir cat's paws and we didn't get too excited about leaving until we were ready.

The cat's paws held and we set the big spinnaker again and went north once more. It was hot and sunny and comfortable early—we took turns at the helm and just glided along. The wind more or less held all day, not much happened except we saw a big cruising powerboat run up on a beach in English Bay, which was fun. We got to the entrance to False Creek in the late afternoon and took the spinnaker down, and the wind started to fill in from the north.

This was a little bit of a problem as False Creek is one of the few places you aren't supposed to sail. It's narrow, it's got crazy boat traffic, it's got a Coast Guard station right there watching everything but the "no wake" rule. We'd rowed in and out of there before but it was too windy for that. So, we took the sails down and "motored" in under bare poles and the incoming tide. Wasn't a problem, we had to drudge a bit with the anchor to get from one anchorage to the next, but we snuck in, dropped a hook, took a stern tie, and thought we'd enjoy the Vancouver night life a bit.

It blew while we were in Vancouver. We didn't care at all.

After a couple of days we felt it was time to leave and head for home. We rowed out of False Creek in the early morning hours on the ebb tide. The people zipping by in the rowing shells stared.

Very little wind all day, but we kept making time somehow. A lot of wallowing around in the straits in a sloppy swell. We kept sailing south all night as the wind was supposed to fill in again. It kept acting like it would and then almost dying. I sailed in the dark for hours and watched the big ships go by.

My buddy took the early watch and the wind came up just before dawn. I awoke to the sounds of water rushing by and a glorious reach. My buddy was tired and said he'd try to sleep, but the wind kept building and soon we were tearing south in rolling four footers and only hitting the high spots. He tried to sleep for a couple of hours and finally gave up. The seastate got pretty rough as the flood tide caught full strength, but the little Vega was fast and didn't care at all. We made great time back to the island where we had spent the night a couple of days before, but as we got within a half mile of the entrance the wind suddenly backed and almost died. We scrambled to change to the big headsail—a pretty strong tide runs across the entrance and we didn't want to get swept by. A few touchy moments and some worry, but we threaded past the reefs and got inside the bay, found a little harbor breeze again and within the hour were tied up and making supper. We were glad for that and were pretty tired.

The next morning we awoke to sun and a 15 knot southeasterly. We set sail and were home in a just couple of hours. It was the weekend and we passed a number of other cruising boats—although just a couple of them were under sail. As I packed the sails away back in the slip I was glad for the choice I made to go without an engine. Having an engine would have made our voyage easy and uneventful. We didn't, so it made it interesting and challenging. I was a bit saddened to see so few people realize that...

Tom Weber

On Choosing One's Sailboat:

So you may have an idea know about the kind of sailboat you need; a sailboat capable of cruising. By cruising I mean: sailing and exploring, I mean going places and seeing new things. I mean sometimes anchoring, sometimes hanging in posh marinas drinking cheap beer, sometimes being tied up under bridge abutments. I mean a boat you can trust in any condition you can psychologically hold up in. I mean what you want: to go where you want to when you want to. There are two ways to do this:

A) Have unlimited funds. Sail what you like. Forget my book.

B) Have a maintainable, workable boat you can afford. Read on.

So here we go.

A SMALL BOAT: You <u>must</u> have a small boat. By this I mean 7000 to 10000 pounds per able–bodied seaman aboard. This may mean just you.

A STRONG BOAT: It cannot be too tough. You're going to sail it hard, and people will bash into it while you're away. It's going to suffer, and it needs to be able to take it.

A CHEAP BOAT: This means you can afford it; to buy it, to use it, to keep it up, and to lose it. It means that there are no systems on board that you cannot understand and keep intact.

First point. I know this is going to be unpopular. Contrary to the yacht press, which now states flatly that one cannot cruise in anything of less than 38 feet in length—small boats are by far the most effective cruisers. By leaps and bounds far. Most of the argument for the big boat masquerades under the guise of seaworthiness, but this is baloney. The main reason that the minimum length of a cruiser has gotten so huge is that the people on them cannot exist without gobs of crazy mechanical systems—thus one needs a huge boat to house the ice-maker. People have come to expect the ability to take a land based life-style to sea with them—this is impossible without making grave compromises to the safety, quality, and performance of the craft.

That dangerous prejudice aside, and addressing the issue of seaworthiness: small boats can be very seaworthy, in fact more so in many circumstances. The size of a boat is a factor in its ultimate seaworthiness, but only one factor, and not one of the more important factors—not nearly so important as, for example, quality of construction. Seaworthiness itself, as I see it, is a factor of safety and not the other way around, but again perhaps not the most important factor here either. One will, or should, face few storms. The storms that one will face likely will not be of a catastrophic magnitude. One could engineer an unsinkable boat—a ballasted steel sphere would be a good start, it would handle the worst storms and stay afloat. But it wouldn't sail worth beans, and on a lee shore would be a terribly unsafe boat. Safety, that attribute of being not likely to hurt you in any way, you then see, is a factor in the effectiveness of one's choice of a boat. Obviously, if one's boat sinks—it's a failure. So is it a failure if it breaks, injures you, and ends your sailing days. So is it a failure if it is too large to comfortably handle. So too is it a failure if it is too heavy to make passages under sail. So too is it a failure if it is too complex and expensive to maintain that you never go anywhere with it. Big boats, regardless of what anyone says, are much less safe than small ones, even IF we admit that they may be less likely to sink in a very few rare circumstances.

Continuing with that thought, let me point out that very few boats sink in any size, and most people who die in boating do so by falling overboard drunk, accidents, and gear failure, in that order. The drunken thing is unavoidable (yeah, I've done it) so we won't talk about it. Accidents, like the poor bastard I just read about, circumnavigator, great sailor, careful prudent seaman, gets run over by a powerboat while snorkeling—these are often unavoidable as well, assuming one lives one's life and doesn't just hide in a padded cell. Be careful, but not too much so; unless we shoot all power boaters on sight this will be a major problem for time to come, but as yet that's still illegal so we'll move on. Gear failure, such that everything was right and something just broke—this is unavoidable as well: no matter how careful one is eventually something is going to booger up. On a small boat, however, loads are small and Norwegian Steam goes a long way towards making them right. On a big boat, however, stuff just rips your arm off.

Not a problem, you think? Ah, voice of a novice! You'll learn your lesson just like everyone else; you'll buy the big boat, you won't be able to handle it—the day job you've got to have to pay for it will keep your body soft as well, it will wear you out on a day sail—and so, you'll do what the petty yachtsmen do. On your allotted yearly weekend you'll motor someplace, find they've got no berthage for your big boat, and you'll motor back. Next year, you'll just stay home. But if you've got an ear to hear, again, read on.

Here's the big obvious bugaboo: ground tackle. As with many things in this world, it is so with good anchors—there ain't no substitute for displacement (this statement makes a excellent mantra, by the way). Among anchors, the primary virtue, their virility, so to speak, is their weight, pure and simple. Sure, as we've said, types and styles have pluses and minuses, sailors like to gas about them, but *heavy is good and don't let anyone tell you otherwise.* Two things cause an anchor to fail. The first is that it drags, meaning that it never got properly set. A heavy anchor sets easier because it simply bites through the grass and crud easier. Secondly, assuming the anchors are set properly, they break. Strong is good, and strong means heavy—pure cross sectional dimensions. Think on this.

On my little 28 foot boat. I have a 20 lb. Bruce with 30 feet of 5/16 BBB chain and 300' of 5/8 nylon for my primary hook and a 12 lb. Bruce with another 30 feet of 5/16 BBB chain and 250 of $^1/_2$ " nylon for my kedge. This is certainly not overkill, most cruisers with experience would say I'm on the light side—for my area, however, it is adequate and practical. Yet the yacht literature will rate this setup as adequate for as much as a 36' 30000 lb. boat! That's 4 times my displacement. Nonsense. I'll tell you why they say that too, because my set up is about the top limit of what a normal guy can drag off the bottom without screwing his back up. This probably 60 to 80 pounds worth full of mud.

Windlass? Well, yes, might be helpful at times, but the mechanical advantage comes from being slow, and sometimes a guy has a need to deal with the hook with alacrity. An anchor is a piece of safety gear, by the way, and all that might stand between you and grief: no power, no wind, no oars, a reef, and a 4 knot current. If you can't deal with it in a rush it is of no use. You may as well leave it at home.

Power windlass? Obviously no good if no power, but it's the thing that allows a lot of people on the water. It's expensive. Can you afford a tow if it buggers up? Can you afford a new boat? I saw a new powerboat go on the rocks just last weekend because of this. Think about it. To rely on a windlass isn't prudent, but neither is it prudent to be on the water uninformed and with unrealistic expectations.

Sinking again. Everyone is really scared about sinking. That's reasonable, but the response to it is not. Sure, the thought of getting the hell beat out of you in a small boat in storm conditions is highly unpleasant. Yes, one can imagine the huge wave coming, here comes the One Wave, and that's it. But the truth is most people, in most boats, survive this event relatively unscathed—assuming that the boat is strong enough to bear the shear impact of the waves. People use this excuse to buy big boats—ignoring the consequences and the reality.

But here's the reality. Most sinking is not caused by the One Wave. It is caused by the collision with some floating object, such as with the One Freight Container. The collision with the freight container is caused by not posting a watch AT ALL TIMES. Not posting a watch at all times is caused by a cruising couple on an all too big boat—loaded with gear and running on autopilot—not possessed with enough stamina to maintain the required four hour on and four hour off sailing routine—let alone handle sail proficiently alone most of the time. Thus, as I read this; big boats *causing* accidents—and thus—less safe.

One other dose of reality. One of the best arguments for big boats is the greater potential speed under sail. Of course they are; this is purely a function of waterline length. This is a legitimate observation, and it is indeed an argument worth thinking through. Within safe parameters—this a big question in itself—a faster boat is indeed safer than a slow one for no reason other than it is less likely to be exposed to hazardous conditions—it spends less time passage making. Contrary currents are also less likely to cause hazards even if one has, by error, found oneself in these conditions.

All of this is true. A large vessel, driven well, with an able crew, will make better, faster passages than a smaller one in ideal circumstances. However, if there is no crew, or the crew is not able to drive the large vessel at the same level of proficiency as the smaller one—this is not the case. If due to crew strength, the large vessel is most often under shortened sail, or is simply not as handy in stays, it will—in practicality—not be faster, and its potential gains in safety will not be realized. Practically speaking, on a short day passage of 50 or so miles, the time it takes to set sail on the bigger boat eats all of the speed potential that it has over the smaller boat. Comparing a 40 footer with my 28–foot boat—in good conditions to weather I might average 5 knots, the large boat 7 knots—though in truth these are both optimistic figures. That makes my passage a 10–hour passage, and the larger boat makes a 7.5 hour passage. The larger boat, however, will take longer to get under-way—by perhaps 15 minutes on either end—making an 8–hour passage. In reality, the wind will shift and change—all of these adjustments destroy the lead of the larger boat. With a short crew, a headsail change or two will make the overall time considerably slower. In light air, definitely so. Downwind, in less than 10 knots of air, which is more common than people think, most all boats are just about the same speed. In reality, large boats are not too often much faster.

If it is too much boat to tack smartly, it is frankly foolhardy to assume one has the capacity to beat off a lee shore. Not seaworthy, nor safe.

Marketing—have you been suckered, you free–thinker you? Every-body is uptight about gales and hurricanes and such. Yes, for sure, this is legitimate. Let me state for the record, however, that somewhere between about 35 and 40 knots lies the point at which most boats, power, sail, traditional or otherwise, won't make way to weather any-more. A lot of them won't make any before that. Truthfully as well, a true 40–knot blow is uncommon save in squalls and can be avoided as long as one sails the proper seasons. One may and expect to see solid 30's the year around, but 40 knots is a lot of wind and can most always be avoided in coastal sailing if one pays attention. The real truth is that most sailing is done at the other end of the scale, in the 0 to 10 knots category. A small smart sloop is always faster than a bigger one in these conditions and far more handy. All of the boats I've personally seen go on the rocks did so in less than 15 knots of air...

Second point: Strong boat. A boat must be strong, so it just doesn't come apart. If you really use your boat, you are going to beat the hell out of it. My boat especially, being engineless—more on that in a moment—sometimes gets driven really hard, and a lot of boats would just fold up. Besides, there's always guys running into you—and I've never seen someone pay up for the damage.

Go around to a few boat yards and take a look around, and count (yes, there will be more than one) the number of new boats that have their keels falling off. You will see not a few with the decks popping off—even those with some high dollar names. Eye the sheer line and see how many come off the ways brand new and hogged—too floppy to take their needed rig tension. Take a look at some plastic classic—the Pearson "Triton" is probably the paradigm example—to see how things really ought to be put together. You will be shocked at how poorly a lot of boats are put together once you start to look. There is absolutely no question that a small rugged boat is terrifically safer than a brand new poorly built boat. Can you afford a well–built 40–foot boat? I doubt it, or you wouldn't be reading my book.

Sub note: A small boat is proportionally much stronger than a large boat and is subject to proportionally much less strain. This is due to the smaller radius of the curvature of the hull, which means it is much stiffer and has less surface area for force to act upon than a large boat will. Chew on this for a bit, it is an interesting study and it means that there is an ideal size for a fiberglass boat where strength, stability, waterline length, displacement, and volume all peak. I'd guess somewhere around 28 to 30 feet.

Third point: A cheap boat. This boat I am describing is not going to be cheap. Good old boats are starting to command real money and are getting hard to find. What I mean by cheap is that there is not a lot of frilly nonsense that takes a lot of time and expenditure to keep up. Keep the gear simple and to a minimum, but of that you have, make it first rate.

Most "sailors" are, for all practical purposes, capable of being stranded indefinitely by nothing more than a dead battery. There is very little virtue in this. An awful lot of boats have such complicated systems that the likelihood of such a failure is quite likely. Of course, this becomes a safety issue. Yes, the presence of every system on board—on a boat that relies on engine power or battery power—is a hazard. They must be highly maintained to not become liabilities.

I think it is reasonable to expect to pay 10% of the value of your boat a year to keep it up. Let me state this a different way—10% of the value of the systems on board—even if the boat isn't worth that much. Even if you don't spend it you must squirrel it away for when you need new sails, etc.

My boat. I've got a 28 foot LOD Pearson "RENEGADE." It's 8'6" on the beam and displaces a shade over 7000lbs in its current trim. It's a William Shaw design, exceedingly well balanced, good looking, and fast even by modern standards. Low aspect Marconi rig, of course, modified full keel with a balanced spade rudder, and I absolutely slaughter all but the most exotic race sleds to weather.

This boat is all go and no nonsense. Again, I'm engineless, so I don't go unless I sail there, but I admit I do break the sweeps out on occasion when it's a flat calm, though mostly just to keep my sanity intact. It is routine for me to average 5 knots as my VMG dead to weather if there is any kind of wind at all, unless it is really choppy; for as with all small boats, big seas are fine and flat is great—but when the lump just about matches your waterline length and you get to hobbyhorse along it really slows you down and is just a hassle. Even though, while it's slow, it's steady—I've bucked along into curling 6 footers for hours dead into a 35 knot blow under my reefed main alone, making about a knot and a half, tacking through 90 degrees. I can't gripe about that. Even pretty dry considering. I don't have a spray dodger, nor feel the need for it.

I love this boat. It was designed with sailors in mind. A huge V–berth forward (over 7 feet) and an enclosed head; two real sea bunks amidships, also well over 6 ft in length. Nothing but necessities. No settee, none of that nonsense. No, it doesn't have standing headroom; no well–proportioned boat can have standing headroom in much under 30 to 35 feet. But am 6'3" so all things are relative. In the cock-pit I've got plenty of headroom.

Forward is a twenty–gallon water tank which is good for me for three weeks. In the old bilge well under where the engine used to be I installed another which holds 35 gallons. That's a lot of water for a little boat. Yes, I know how to ration water; but my wandering skills were developed as a backpacker and not as a yachtsman so I'm perhaps a bit more frugal (when you carry it you get frugal quick.) No, I don't have a shower on board. When asked what I do, I say that I don't get dirty—only half in jest. Another skill learned as a backpacker. You can always tell the neophyte because he's covered with mud all the way to his eyebrows.

There's a good deal of stowage V–berth that is largely empty. In the cabin there used to be a little propane furnace rigged with a blower that sucks air off the cabin sole. The back side of the tile lined box it lived in protruded into the hanging locker which warmed up the clothes in there and kept things dry. I also used to have a little propane cook top. I've since changed all this after a lot of thought and I'll tell you why. The propane heater was effective, but barely, and in the long WET winters we have in the Puget Sound it encouraged it to rain inside. I really wanted something else, but everything I saw was far too expensive, heavy, and big. I like diesel heaters, but they all stink and I didn't want to install another fuel tank. I didn't want a diesel stove because they are hotter than hell to use in the summer—big and heavy again. I really like propane for fuel; it is clean, hot, and cheap—and safer than most people think as long as one is reasonably careful. Diesel explodes too, by the way, it just takes a bit more work to get it to that point—but less than you think.

So what I did was fabricate a dual fuel stove. Propane/ solid fuel. It is basically a little potbellied wood cook stove with incinerator burners in it, built really heavy so they don't burn out. It works great. The propane burners are right under the stove top so I can lift the plates and put a spider on them and use it just like a regular propane top, or I can leave the tops on and heat up the whole thing. It draws great so no moisture in the cabin, just clean, dry heat. I can fill it up with driftwood and light off the propane; in five minutes I've got a wood fire and I shut the propane off. I also dump all my boat trash and even food scraps and junk in it and burn it all off. It really works well. I watch it like a hawk, however, because its got no thermocouples nor any of that other crap that screws up and blows up boats—because it tricks you into not paying attention. Pretty spiffy. It sure works for me. I've got enough sense to always shut the propane off when I leave the boat. The valve is in the cockpit—one's got no excuse not to.

I did insulate the entire interior above the waterline as well. What I did is buy the closed–cell urethane foam like they make backpacking ground pads out of, and contact cemented it to the inside of the hull. Boy, was that a jolly sort of job! I remember I had only one sorry little cheap beer with me that day—I had been nursing it along—and at one point I was shocked at how buzzed I was. Wear a respirator. Dead brain cells aside, this made a total transformation of the boat. It was amazing how much more comfortable things became. The last thing I did was sew little booties out of that polar fleece stuff that I can stick over the inside of my ports to keep them from sweating. I'd encourage that too.

Electronics: I've got the basics, but electronics are cheap and handy nowadays, as long as one buys good units and no those with a dozen silly features on them which serve no purpose but to jack up the price and make the key pad functions more awkward. I've got Loran, GPS, VHF, depth and a big stereo system. It would be tough to not have any of those. I've also had wind gauges and a speed log, which are cool but next to useless. The boat came with those. I tore them off and pitched them once I realized their value.

For electricity I've got a single 78–watt solar panel which keeps the batteries up. In the winter it gets a bit tight for a coupe of months but I usually hang out at marinas during this time anyway so no big deal. I've got two 220amp hour 6–volt golf cart batteries for juice, this has always seemed like enough.

I've got lots of tools and supplies on board; lots of goops, glues, and paints. The most of my tools are those terrible garbage Chinese things they sell for near to nothing. I figure they're disposable and it doesn't bother me to loan them.

I've got two 1.2 foot ash sweeps stowed on the cabin house—they look good there and give me something to stand on up there when I'm hard on it. I've got big oarlocks rigged in case I need to row, or scull, or if I should lose the rudder.

All ports open forward; both hatches dog down; the forward hatch is watertight—as in submergible, watertight.

Sounds like a very fine, traditional little boat, does it not? And yes it is—yet it is time to make a care point on tradition—"tradition" for tradition's sake is more often a swindle than not—and it is very important we pay attention to what we are looking at. If traditional means "historically proven to be functional and reliable" then I am happy with that. Yes, I will agree. If traditional means "having a quaint character" then I certainly do not. One must be on guard for the swindles...

Speaking of swindles: The Golden Age of Sail. This myth is a lie from the pit of hell. Most of the tradition of the sea has been that of horrible punishing hardship; that of short, mean lives—that of drudgery, slavery, buggery, lashings, poor health, and constant danger. Broken mast, broken spars, battered sails flinging broken men off into black eternity. Jeez! Forget that crap. So much of the fashionable literature masquerading as sea stories about this era absolutely neglects the thousands of men who suffered and died as veritable slaves on ships—but it was these men, not the fool in the funny outfit on the poop deck—that made it happen. To suggest otherwise is a terrible affront. Thankfully most of that is over with.

There was, however, a Golden Age of Sail, but one that gets very little press time, likely because its message is not commercially viable. This was the era of offshore racing between the end of WWII and the mid–1960s. This is when a bunch of crazy fellows who came home from the war and decided that after they'd been shot at for a few years they'd never quite fit in again in normal society, so they took to sailing little boats at breakneck speeds all over the globe. Little, little boats too—folkboats, that kind of thing—half the size of my RENEGADE. Most of the time these guys were broke or close to it; most of the boats they had, in spite of the homage paid to them, range from the "nothing special" to frankly trash—most of these boats didn't sail so hot but the men in them certainly did. Bruce, Coles, Hasler, etc. these kind of guys. Pretty great bunch. Read their stuff. One can learn from them.

The primary lesson that these guys preach is this—*CREW!* The heart of a boat is its crew. A well–crewed boat, even if the boat is not really up to the challenge, comes through again and again. Crew: but this lesson is lost on us because it doesn't sell. You can't just walk down to the corner marine store and buy character. You can, however, buy a life raft. Think of this—no doubt law will soon require boats to carry EPIRBS as well as the mountains of safety gear many places already require—but almost no one requires any indicator of ability to operate a boat. Makes lots of sense, right? It is no mystery to me what people want to hear—people want to hear that you can work your whole life in as a Tax Auditor or some other bastard position—bleed enough money off of poor ignorant people to buy a yacht, and sail away to points unknown expecting to have a glorious experience. Let me tell you—most people who do this don't. They have a miserable time. The harbors of this world are littered with big "ocean–going" yachts littered with cruising gear—that have made one passage and that was it. The "for sale" sign hangs grimly.

Let me be straight about it. Unless you've go about 1 pound of able–bodied sailor on board for every 50 pounds displacement, you are under crewed and not seaworthy. Period. Your safety and success is then dependent, with no recourse, on mechanical systems that take the place of a pair of hands—you are dependent, as well, on the poor grunt you built your boat on minimum wage, installed these systems, and frankly hates your guts for your perceived affluence and privilege—jus-tified or no. Besides this—you must read able–bodied and sailor here, unskilled clumsy sorts, asleep sorts, or incapacitated sorts, don't count—in fact you need to add them to the weight side of the equation. They are more likely to freak out or get injured during a crisis than be any help, thus increasing the magnitude of the crisis.

But, you say, what about the legions of gray haired sorts cruising the world, in their Wondrous 50's? How many of them drown? Very few, but pay attention. First of all, there are far fewer of them than you might think. Those that are out there are only successful because A: they've got enough money to buy and maintain labor saving devices, and this is a huge chunk of money; and B: they motor most everywhere; and C: the weather has been relatively nice and predictable for the last 20 years. This is all about to change. First, while some people can afford a $500,000 boat, the $50,000 a year to maintain it, $10,000 a year in insurance, and $2500 a month or more to cruise it, very few people can, especially retire early and do that. Secondly, fuel prices are bound to got through the roof, and many of the little undeveloped ports of the world where people want to go will be forced to ration fuel—this sort of sailing is very fuel intensive, and simply will be impossible at some point in the future. Lastly, global warming is a fact, any sailor knows it, out storm seasons are gong to be far longer and more severe than they've been in the past. Even in harbors, one might say especially in harbors, crises happen, and it just takes meat to deal with them. Many of these people expect good–natured help from other cruisers during these times of difficulty, but this generosity has really worn thin. Beware, if you ask someone to handle a line for you they've got a salvage claim and rightly so.

So my point is this; this era of boat cruising is nearing its close. No question about it. That doesn't mean one has to stay home—but I'll be frank, friend, because I want you to succeed—if you're starting from scratch today you're probably 4 to 5 years out before you're off to Fiji. Better think ahead, and keep an eye to weather. One most likely won't be able to buy oneself into this lifestyle for much longer, and once again one will have to earn one's way along by skill and self–reliance.

Conclusions

So again, why an engineless boat?

The first reason is that straight sailboats are just a lot more interesting.

Most of us choose an engineless boats because to a lot of us the "experience" of sailing is important. It might be more important than the destination of where we sail to. This is an important attitude of a sailor. People talk about being at the mercy of the wind and water, so do we; but that's probably overblown. The truth of the matter is that a well planned voyage comes off without a hitch most of the time. I cruise with other boats—even those with (gasp!) engines. More often than not, I'm to our next port first, not last. Still, there are times in which things just don't cooperate. Other than turn on the engine and fix the issue—we get a "learning experience" that we call "playing sailor". If we do learn the lesson, it is unlikely that it happens again. Again—the inconveniences of sailing without engine assist are a good part of the reason we do it. With the risk of sounding silly—the truth is that sailing is pretty easy to do—unless it's hard. Since most guys rob themselves of the opportunity to partake of what going to sea is all about—mostly that hard stuff—they never learn to make the fine decisions that separate a skilled boat handler from the rest. If you're going to sail an boat with no help from an engine—we guarantee you're going to get a lot of practice in these matters, like it or not. Again, to a lot of us that's at the core of the appeal.

One gets a sense of satisfaction out of an activity in direct proportion to the amount of sweat that went into it to make it happen. Sailing involves more sweat than motor–sailing. I've said this before and it offends some folks—but I think the comparison is valid. No one would confuse mountaineering with riding chair lifts. No one would confuse driving up the eastern seaboard with hiking the Appalachian Trail. Neither should people confuse "sailing" with "motorsailing". Not that "sailing" is that big of a deal—but for that matter, neither is hiking. The key to hiking, mountaineering, and *sailing*—when one actually does it—is that these all often involve *a lot of discomfort and hard work*. It's pretty clear why "engineless sailors" irritate some people so much—we shoot holes in the status and elitism that the yacht world so much wants to claim. The dirty little secret of the sailing world is that *most people that own sailboats don't like to sail*. They like the status that they think "being a sailor" gives them, but they don't like to sail. They especially don't like the hard parts of sailing—beating to weather, headsail changes, being wet and cold: engines, roller furling, spray dodgers? Yes indeed, many people get into sailing for *no other reason* than the idea that owning a sailboat somehow conveys status—and they want that status. They want the status among others, but aren't too interested in the "sweat" aspect that might give them internal satisfaction, which to us, anyway, is far more important. Well, among most of the population, one wouldn't be given much status about driving a car down the east coast. Even in a community of drivers that want to sit around and gloat about their driving—an occasional guy that walked the same trek would start to make that activity look pretty silly—not that it really matters anyhow. I think that most people in this world view "sailing" or "motorsailing" or any of that crap as a peculiar sort of self–grandizement and one doesn't get any status from doing it even if one cared. Best not to care—one is bound to be disappointed.

All right, we've talked enough about that baloney. Let's talk about the last and very convincing, very important reason to ditch the engine. A very, very, valid and practical reason…

Sailing a boat without the aid of an engine is far, far, far cheaper.

Let's be clear. People think sailboats are powered by wind. This is not true. They are powered by money. It is simply a fact that person A with income X leaves sooner and goes further in a less expensive boat than in a more expensive one. Do you have income X minus 1 and want to leave now? Our way may be your only way. Time to face facts and buckle down.

Now for the numbers. Pay attention. This is going to shock you.

It is pretty reasonable to expect that the cost and maintenance of a marine diesel engine is going to run fully half of the maintenance cost of the entire boat. This doesn't seem like a really big deal if the boat sits at the dock all the time—like most do—and rots into the water. But we're not talking about that. We're talking about a boat that goes places and is used hard. I think you'll blow the rig, engine, and sails out of a boat every 5 years if you're cruising hard. I build my own sails and I can get by relatively cheap on that, but the engine is a tough one. I can rebuild engines, sure—but fixing a marine diesel engine is ridiculously expensive—parts are terrible, you'll have complicated yard time. If you can't fix stuff yourself in a big way—repowering is going to cost you multiples of thousands of dollars. To put a new diesel engine in my 28 foot boat it would cost me upward of 6000 bucks. I can pretty well cruise for a year on that...

Suppose then, you tear the engine out. Now a whole new set of issues present themselves. By removing the engine—you have removed the heart of the modern cruising boat. Without the aid of the engine—most modern "necessities" that boats carry simply won't work for you. There is no way you can possibly generate the power needed for watermakers, nor radar, nor SSB, nor refrigeration, nor even some depth finders, nor even a diesel stove a lot of the time. Not having all this crap saves you a phenomenal amount of money as well, in fact, not having an engine simply prohibits the use of a lot of this gear. I do see boats decked up like space probes with panels and generators and stuff—I get asked about the viability of that sort of thing—I've come to respond with this: "unnecessary windage." You don't need that junk—there are all sorts of alternatives—and we'll show you how to run a boat with NO electrical power if you'd like. Starting there, add reasonable technology for a reasonable amount of comfort…but pay big attention to the next point.

The next big point is this: a "cruising" sailboat must carry a certain amount of gear on board. It must carry a certain amount of fuel, water, sails, repair supplies and tools, a tender, clothing, extra line, ground tackle, etc,. On a small boat, this can take up an impractical amount of room—and you see the kind of boats that look like the "Grapes of Wrath" gone to sea. Now certainly—the amount of gear one needs is often overstated—and a good amount of skill can reduce this amount to a large degree, but somewhere there is a bottom line of what one can carry and still be properly equipped. This argument persuades a lot of people to buy bigger boats than they can afford——a catastrophe!

Take a look at what happens when you remove an engine, however. You gain a HUGE amount of stowage. On my boat, the engine compartment took up about 60 cubic feet of stowage space. The engine, tank, hoses, and all other assorted gear ran into nearly a thousand pounds. That's enough size and weight for carrying all the gear for a serious ocean passage. One gains a cargo hold—located in the ideal place—and of an ideal size and shape in many cases. In other words, an engineless 28 foot boat might have the carrying capacity of a 32 foot boat with an engine in…this makes smaller boats FAR more functional than they would be otherwise.

PERFORMANCE: You cannot believe what taking an inboard engine out of a sailboat does for its performance. The change is jaw-dropping. I'll run quickly through a few numbers to show as to why, which demystifies(and validates) things a bit—but it is such a big deal that I don't see why more people don't talk about it.

On my boat:

Removing the engine raised the boat an 1.5 inches on her marks. That's almost 6 square feet of wetted surface area. It lowered the center of gravity about 2 inches, vastly improving its stability. Removing the prop and strut most likely removed 70% of the hull's drag—hard to believe this; but the data shows that a round strut, three feet long and an inch in diameter generates as much drag as the ENTIRE HULL OF A THIRTY FOOT BOAT! What did it mean in performance? 1.5 knots on every point of sail and 5–8 degrees of pointing. I think that's pretty reasonable to expect and every boat that I've torn the engine out of has gotten close to that in gains. What it really means as well is that a boat without an engine hardly ever needs one…

So what I see is this. A 28 foot sailboat has as much stowage as a 32 foot motorsailor, it goes as fast as a 32 foot motorsailor dragging a screw—it is much less work to sail—you're far more likely to have anchorage or moorage available when you get to port—moorage is just that much cheaper all the time…

A quality, outfitted, engineless 28 foot boat can be put together for less than 20 thousand dollars including all the gear for extended ocean passages. A quality, outfitted 32 foot boat would be tough to have for less than 80 thousand dollars. Sounds to me like if you pull the engine you get the circumnavigation for free…or maybe a couple of them! What I'm getting at is this—all in all, I see one saving perhaps three quarters of the cost of purchase and of cruising by going engineless once everything is considered. Take note!

So now, I've got to counter the objections. I hear this all the time—that having an engine is a safety issue, not an economic or aesthetic issue. I usually hear it with a bit of a snort. I reply: Safety against what? Seriously, against what? Against anything that skill should not have been the first safety aid? With the skill to avoid the problem, what need is there for the engine? I will admit that the engine is a powerful aid to incompetence—but as such in my eyes perpetuates incompetence—and so is a safety issue in itself. When one realizes that the presence of the engine carries inherent hazards with it—increased risk of fire, asphyxiation, injury by mechanical parts, through–hull failure, or even the cases I've read about where the prop strut came undone and the whirling propeller chopped holes in the bottom of the boat—when one realizes that the presence of the engine GREATLY impairs a boats sailing ability and its ability to claw off a lee shore in a gale—it is pretty tough to look at the engine as helping with safety much at all.

The engine issue is one of convenience and comfort. It takes a lot, if not most of the work out of sailing. It does allow one to be in the harbor on schedule, for cocktails, when one could not have entered without under some conditions. But we've already talked about this, some people don't get into sailing for convenience. If convenience is a big deal to you—why take up sailing? What on earth is supposed to be convenient about sailing?

Most of you could sell your car, and with that money, have the means to see the world.

If this rings your bell, let us know.

Afterword

If you really like this sort of thing, and are intrigued by the whole sailing motif, I'd encourage you to check out The Oar Club on the world wide web. The Oar Club is a sailing club dedicated to people who sail real sailboats—at the time of this publication we were about 500 members worldwide and growing. No, you don't have to buy into my flaky philosophy—but you must have a passion for sail, and know what sailing is. You'll not find a more skilled, experienced, and pleasant group of sailors anywhere else. We can be found at **www.oarclub.org**. We offer classes, training, crew positions—we build sails and fix boats—help with pretty much anything that is involved with running a sailboat can be found there. So far, and hopefully forever we've also found the means to keep money and funding out of it and offer all this for FREE to any good person that comes our way. If you're not a sailor, but you'd like to be, this is the way to get a hold of us…

About the Author

Jerome FitzGerald has written numberous articles on sailing and currently cruises his engineless sailboat on the West Coast of the United States.

0-595-21733-8

Printed in the United States
1160700005B/97-98